INSTANT POT
DUO CRISP
AIR FRYER
COOKBOOK

Over
200
Easy Instant Pot Air Fryer
Crisp Recipes for
Beginners and
Advanced User

Louis Witte

Table of Content

Introduction

L et me begin with a confession. I'm an obsessed foodie with a sweet tooth who used to hog on food. And the result was not so happy, because of the criticism I used to face due to the body shape. Next came the tears and struggles to lose weight. Watching the weighing machine every single day, torturing myself with those exercises in the gym, and trying out the hundreds of fad diets I came across, and then the realization hit me on a fine day.

Maintaining a healthy weight and keeping yourself fit and healthy need not be a herculean task. You can have a simple solution – what goes in is what comes out. Ultimately what is getting stored in your body is the food that you feed your body. I go by the famous quotes of Hippocrates, "Let food be your medicine and let medicine be your food."

Here onward, I started my experiments with food. The love for healthy eating made me take up a short-term course in Nutrition & Dietetics. Exploring more on food and cooking, I realized that cooking is both an art and science. Food should be tasty to tempt the family, including the picky eaters. At the same time, it should cook in a way by minimizing the presence of unhealthy fats while retaining healthy fats and nutritional values.

I know what you must be thinking. It's a tough feat to achieve. Don't worry; we are on the same page on this. You must be wondering how to accomplish the task. Don't get surprised, let me introduce to you my best friend in healthy cooking – the Instant Pot Duo Crisp 11-in-1 Air Fryer, a fantastic cooking appliance with dual cooking function and various features. You can do multiple forms of air fry and pressure cook.

It cooks crispy fry with low oil or nil oil. Wondering how? Well, hot air does the trick. I have recommended my friends to switch to the air fryer, and all of them are happy with the results.

The Instant Pot Duo Crisp Air Fryer Cookbook targets all those beautiful people who love fried foods (just like me), but wish to avoid unhealthy fats. In this book, I have put together a collection of 80 mouth-watering recipes for you to try with the air fryer.

Each recipe has been tested, and trust me, they are yummy! You are going to have a hard time keeping your kids away from these crispy fries. Air fryers are easy to use, and these recipes are fast and can cook in less than 30 minutes. You can cook almost anything with the air fryer, which is much faster and healthier than the traditional way of cooking.

The collection of recipes I have compiled in this book covers all your cooking needs, from breakfast to lunch, snacks, and dinner. You can find 80 healthy recipes divided into Breakfast & Brunch, Fish & Seafood, Beef lamb & Pork, Poultry, Vegetarian & Vegan, Desserts, Snacks & Appetizers that are delectable and easy to cook. These recipes come best when prepared using Instant Pot Air Fryer Duo Crisp Cooking Appliance. It is my personal favorite, and I love the texture of corns and peanuts when roasted in Instant Pot. It features with an 'instant crisp technology' and multi-level basket along with a dehydrating – broiling tray to make juicy, crispy food.

So, let's get started with air fryer cooking. Turn the pages and choose your favorite recipes.

Chapter 1 The Basics of Instant Pot Duo Crisp Air Fryer

With the 11-in-1 function, the Instant Pot Duo Crisp Air Fryer has made cooking and living easier for every household. It holds with the impeccable features of 'set and forget' functions. The basic function of the Instant Pot is just like any other cooking appliance. Still, in this version, it comes with both pressure cooker and air fry options, which is made possible with the help of two separate lids, the crisp lid for air frying and pressure cook lid for pressure cooking – fast and easy, all by simply changing the covers.

With such ease, you will have all the cooking methods available over the control panel of this Instant Pot. The pressure cook lid offers you the function of six wet cooking options like PRESSURE COOK, STEAM, SAUTÉ, SLOW COOK, WARM, and SOUS VIDE. Similarly, in the air fryer function, it offers you the option to AIR FRY, BAKE, ROAST, BROIL, and DEHYDRATE. Since the cookbook is all about air fry recipes, you can find exclusive features of Instant Pot Duo Crisp Air Fryer.

The selection for the function is effortless using the soft-touch options as needed, without twisting any knobs or rotating switches. It comes with smart and manual cooking options for air frying. When you select the smart cooking options in the Air Fry segment, it will choose the default temperature setting, and you need to select the required cooking time manually. However, air frying processing will not begin without pressing the START option.

The quick and smart program makes it easy for everyone to use it, from a naïve cook to a professional chef, for preparing healthy meals. The device comes with a bright LED and control panel that is easy to identify and use. The readable icons can give you a clear cooking status and help you to maneuver the device accordingly, making it simple to open, flip, and close with ease even while you are cooking.

It also offers you to customize the cooking options, setting time and save the setting as your favorite or regular meals so that whenever you repeat a recipe, the Instant Pot will remember the temperature and time for the dish, thus saving you the time and energy. With the bonus of the DELAY START button, you can now ensure that your dinner is ready when you want it to and not prior to that. The KEEP WARM feature will also help the dish stay warm. Sounds like a helping hand in the kitchen, right?

Highlights of the Instant Pot Duo Crisp Air Fryer

The Instant Pot Duo Crisp Air Fryer weighs around 22 pounds and comes with a large display control panel, which has positioned facing the user. Let's look at some specifications of this product:

❀ The Instant Pot comes with two lids; one is the pressure-cooking lid, and the other an air fryer crisp lid. The crisp air fryer lid comes with an inbuilt power lid that charges the pot and provides the connection without having to use any external power for the Instant Pot.

❀ The Instant Pot also comes with a safe launch pad called the protective pad that can use to store the air fryer lid. Once you've cooked, you don't want to keep the cover on the countertop of your kitchen; thus, comes the protective pad, which automatically helps the lid in cooling down and releasing any moisture.

A Quick Tip: You can always reverse the protective pad, and it will convert as the cover lid for the air fryer. You must place the air fryer lid over the protective pad and turn it to the right, and it will lock the lid, thus working as a cover.

❀ In the pressure cooker lid, you will find a button at the top, which works as a pressure release valve. Unlike the previous version of the Instant Pot, you won't have to press and hold the nob to release the steam. Instead, you can just press the button, and it will release the steam and pressure. Once done, it will automatically make a 'click' sound, and the button will recoil to its original position, thus alerting that the pressure has released.

❀ The Instant Pot Duo Crisp Air Fryer also comes with an extra condensation cup that can attach to the sides of the appliance to collect any dripping. You can remove it, dump the dripping and place it back on the cooker to avoid any liquid get released from the appliance.

❀ The Instant Pot air fryer comes with an inner liner pot, which is mandatorily required to place in the pot before preparing for any dish. None of the air fryer functions will work without the inner pot placed in the appliance. If you try cooking without the inner pot, the control panel will notify you that you must place the inner pot. The feature is ideal for supporting clean and safe cooking.

- The Instant Pot also comes with a trivet called the multi-functional rack that allows you easy cooking. You can either fold it upside down or downside, as needed. The trivet has 3 separations that will help you to fold it as needed before you can use it for cooking.

- The Air Fryer pot also offers a basket for a quick, crispy meal. You can use this basket to crisp your recipe, use certain dishes as needed.

- In case you're dehydrating, broiling, or just frying, you can make use of the separator that comes with the Instant Pot Air Fryer known as the broil/dehydrating tray or the separator. Since the air fryer lid blows hot air from the fan behind the electric coil of the convection lid, the separator ensures closer cooking for a crisp dish.

- In case if you use the wrong lid, the control panel will alert you like a ping on display. For example: If you use the pressure-cooker lid for any function of air fryer, the appliance won't work; instead, it will first ask you to change the cover.

- The 'instant crisp technology' ensures to provide you with a juicy, tender, and crispy meal with a golden finish, with little or no oil, thus making every dish a unique and healthy one.

Functions and Applications

Air Fryer: In this mode, you will have to use the crisp lid, instead of the pressure cooker lid. The function helps in frying the meals depending upon the temperature and time requirement. You can select the temperature after pressing on AIR FRY,' and set/change the temperature and the time that you wish to cook and then press to START for beginning the cooking.

- Default temperature: 400°F / 204°C
- Temperature range: 180°F – 400°F / 82°C – 204°C
- Suggested use: Fresh / Frozen fries, chicken wings or shrimps
- Default cooking time: 00:18
- Cooking time range: 00:01 – 01:00

Roast: In this function, there is no pre-set, you can choose the temperature, and the time you require to roast your meal or dish and press START to begin the cooking process. Once you have maintained the temperature and the time, the Instant Pot will remember the pre-set in case if you wish to cook the same dish again.

* Default temperature: 380°F / 193°C
* Temperature range: 180°F – 400°F / 82°C – 204°C
* Suggested use: Beef, Lamb, Pork, Poultry, Vegetables, Scalloped potatoes & more
* Default cooking time: 00:40
* Cooking time range: 00:01 – 01:00

Bake: Using the air fryer lid, you can bake any dish that you want. The function remains the same, choose the temperature and the time and hit START to begin the baking process. Make sure to have the lid over the launching or cooling pad when you have finished the baking.

* Default temperature: 365°F / 185°C
* Temperature range: 180°F – 400°F / 82°C – 204°C
* Suggested use: Fluffy and light cakes, pastries, and buns.
* Default cooking time: 00:30
* Cooking time range: 00:01 – 01:00

Broil: In the BROIL option, the appliance comes with a 400°F default temperature setting, which you cannot change. Since it's a broiling option and it is the hottest setting, you can only change the time. Only after pressing the START option, the cooking will begin.

* Default temperature: 400°F / 204°C
* Temperature range: Not adjustable
* Suggested use: Nachos, Onion Soup, Malt cheese, etc.
* Default cooking time: 00:08
* Cooking time range: 00:01 – 00:40

De-hydrate: Just like any other pre-set, this one is also changeable, where you can change the temperature and timer as needed before you begin the process to DE-HYDRATE the meal.

❁ Default temperature: 125°F / 52°C

❁ Temperature range: 105°F – 165°F / 41°C – 74°C

❁ Suggested use: Fruit leather, jerky, dried vegetables etc.

❁ Default cooking time: 07:00

❁ Cooking time range: 01:00 – 72:00

Pressure cook: In this setting, it doesn't allow you to choose the temperature as the built-in option available are the frequencies of HIGH and LOW. By clicking on the pressure cook button, you can select the frequency, choose the time for the meal preparation, and hit START. Ensure to change the lid to the pressure cooker lid; otherwise, the control panel will refuse to begin the process.

❁ **Pressure level:** LO (low – 5.8 to 7.2 psi) / HI (high – 10.2 to 11.6 psi)

❁ Suggested use: LO – Fish and seafood, Soft vegetables, rice. HI – Eggs, meat, poultry, roots, hard vegetables, oats, beans, grains, bone broth, chili.

❁ Default cooking time – LO – 00:35 / HI – 00:30

❁ Cooking time range: 00:00 – 04:00

Sauté: Under this function, it provides high or low-frequency operation and timer control. To begin the sauté, select the settings and press START.

* Temperature level: LO (low) / HI (high)
* Suggested use: LO – simmer, reduce, thicken, and caramelize. HI – pan sear, stir fry, sauté & brown.
* Default cooking time – 00:30
* Cooking time range: 00:01 – 00:30

Slow Cook: The function is useful when you wish to slow cook the dishes. The timer of this function can go beyond 24 hours as per the recipe requirement, and the frequencies provided shall be either high or low as per the cooking requirements.

* Temperature level: LO (low) / HI (high)
* Suggested use: LO – All day cooking can set for 6 hours for the best results. HI – faster slow cooking.
* Default cooking time – 06:00
* Cooking time range: 00:30 – 24:00

Steam: It is an ideal option when you wish to steam your dish like rice or dumplings, etc. The pre-set continues to remain the same with the frequency of high or low, and the timer can decide the steaming requirement.

Sous Vide: It is an ideal method for cooking the dish in the Instant Pot for non-fry cooking, which is especially useful for vacuum-sealed food cooking at a precise temperature for an extended period.

* Default temperature: 56°C / 133°F
* Default cooking time – 03:00
* Cooking time range: 00:30 – 99:30

The Control Panel

The control panel of the Instant Pot Duo Crisp Air Fryer is very easy to read and comprehend. Though the LED is small, the displays are easy to read, and interface navigation between the functions are relatively simple. Let us look at some quick highlights of the control panel that can help you understand the device better:

✿ The time format on the control panel displays hours on the left and minutes on the right of the colon. Once the timer hits below 1 minute, the right side of the colon indicates the seconds remaining to complete the cooking.

✿ Once the timer goes off, you will automatically see the light on the KEEP WARM button that will keep your food warm until you are back to check the cooker.

✿ The control panel has no pre-sets; however, if you cook a specific dish multiple times, you can add it as a favorite pre-set to have the same function and settings every time you cook that meal.

✿ On the control panel, you will see a button for DELAY START, which you can use if you want to cook a little later. It will ensure that the dish only cooks when you hit the START button, and until then, the panel will save your settings.

✿ In case, if you want to cancel the meal preparation or wish to add or remove anything from the dish, you can always select the CANCEL button on the control panel, and the Instant Pot will immediately stop the cooking procedure.

✿ The left side of the display is for the temperature setting. You can adjust the temperature by using the plus or the minus button.

✿ On the right side of the display is for the timer. With the help of the plus and the minus button, you can change the timer setting.

✿ The LED is a small black screen that appears on the control panel with blue scripts that signifies the settings you are using and also alerts if any of the devices/functions are missing in the Instant Pot.

Cleaning and Maintenance

Always clean the Instant Pot Duo Crisp Air Fryer after each use. Every part required to clean differently. Please find the chart beneath to understand the process of cleaning.

★ **TIP:** Always ensure that the device is unplugged and is at room temperature before cleaning.

Part	Instruction	Cleaning Method
Accessories ❀ Steam rack ❀ Condensation collector ❀ Air fryer basket base ❀ Protective pad and storage cover ❀ Broil/Dehydration tray	❀ Do not use harsh chemicals, detergent, powder or scouring pads ❀ Use non-stick cooking spray on the tray and air fryer basket for easy cleaning. ❀ Place on the top racks if you are using a machine to clean up ❀ Empty and clean the condensation collector after every use	Dish wash or hand wash
Pressure Cooker Lid & Parts ❀ Anti-block shield ❀ Steam release Handle ❀ Float valve ❀ Sealing ring ❀ Silicone cap	❀ Use mild dish soap to clean up after every use ❀ Place on top rack in the dishwasher ❀ Clean the insides of the steam release pipe ❀ Keep the sealing ring in a ventilated area to avoid any residual odor of flavored meals ❀ For odors, you can add a cup of water, a cup of white vinegar in the inner pot, and run pressure cook for 5 to 10 minutes.	Dish wash or hand wash
Inner Pot	❀ In case of hard water staining, rub the pot with light hands using some vinegar on a sponge. ❀ For burned food residue, soak it in hot water.	Dish wash or hand wash

As a standard cleaning protocol, always make sure to unplug the Instant Pot Duo Crisp Air Fryer before you plan to clean. Similarly, make sure to cool down the appliance; otherwise, it will be a reason for the malfunction and sometimes fail to meet the warranty requirements.

Chapter 2 Breakfast

Egg Bites with Cheese (Pressure Cook)

Prep time: 5 minutes | Cook time: 10 minutes | Serves 2 to 4

- 1 cup filtered water
- 6 eggs
- ½ cup shredded full-fat Cheddar cheese
- ½ cup bell peppers, finely chopped
- ½ cup spinach, finely chopped
- ½ teaspoon dried cilantro
- ½ teaspoon kosher salt
- ½ teaspoon freshly ground black pepper
- Cooking spray

1. Place the trivet in the bottom of your Instant Pot and add the water.
2. Mix together the eggs, cheese, bell peppers, spinach, cilantro, salt, and pepper in a large bowl. Stir well.
3. Spritz a silicone egg mold with cooking spray and ladle the mixture into the impressions in the mold.
4. Put the mold on the trivet with a sling and wrap loosely in aluminum foil.
5. Secure the lid and select Press the Pressure Cook on the Instant Pot and set the cooking time for 10 minutes at High Pressure.
6. When the timer beeps, use a quick pressure release. Carefully open the lid.
7. Remove the egg mold from the pot. Remove the foil and allow to cool for 5 minutes.
8. Scoop the egg bites out of the mold with a spoon and transfer to a serving dish. Serve.

Pumpkin Oatmeal (Pressure Cook)

Prep time: 5 minutes | Cook time: 10 minutes | Serves 6

- 3 cups water
- 1½ cups 2% milk
- 1¼ cups steel-cut oats
- 3 tablespoons brown sugar
- 1½ teaspoons pumpkin pie spice
- 1 teaspoon ground cinnamon
- ¾ teaspoon salt
- 1 (15-ounce / 425-g) can solid-pack pumpkin

1. Place all the ingredients except the pumpkin into the Instant Pot and stir to incorporate.
2. Secure the lid. Select the Pressure Cook and set the cooking time for 10 minutes at High Pressure.
3. Once cooking is complete, do a natural pressure release for 10 minutes, then release any remaining pressure. Carefully open the lid.
4. Add the pumpkin and stir well. Allow the oatmeal to sit for 5 to 10 minutes to thicken. Serve immediately.

Cheesy Arugula Frittata (Pressure Cook)

Prep time: 5 minutes | Cook time: 5 minutes | Serves 2

- 3 eggs, beaten
- ¼ cup loosely packed arugula
- ¼ red onion, chopped
- ¼ cup feta cheese crumbles
- ¼ teaspoon garlic powder
- Kosher salt, to taste
- Freshly ground black pepper, to taste
- 1 cup water

1. Stir together the eggs, arugula, onion, feta cheese crumbles, garlic powder, salt, and pepper in a medium bowl. Pour the egg mixture into a greased round cake pan and cover with foil.
2. Add the water and trivet to the Instant Pot, then place the cake pan on top of the trivet.
3. Lock the lid. Select the Pressure Cook and set the cooking time for 5 minutes at High Pressure.
4. Once cooking is complete, do a natural pressure release for 10 minutes, then release any remaining pressure. Carefully open the lid.
5. Let the frittata rest for 5 minutes in the pan before cutting and serving.

Breakfast Quinoa Salad (Pressure Cook)

Prep time: 15 minutes | Cook time: 1 minute | Serves 4

- 2 cups quinoa, rinsed well

Salad:
- 1 (15-ounce / 425-g) can chickpeas, drained and rinsed
- 1 cucumber, diced
- 1 cup chopped flat-leaf parsley
- ¼ cup extra-virgin olive oil
- 1 red onion, diced
- 1 red bell pepper, diced
- 2 cups vegetable or chicken broth

- 3 cloves garlic, minced
- Juice of 2 lemons
- 2 tablespoons red wine vinegar
- Salt and pepper, to taste
- 1 to 2 cups crumbled feta cheese (optional)

1. Place the quinoa and broth into the Instant Pot and stir to incorporate.
2. Lock the lid. Select the Pressure Cook and set the cooking time for 1 minute at High Pressure.
3. Once cooking is complete, do a natural pressure release for 10 minutes, then release any remaining pressure. Carefully open the lid.
4. Fluff the quinoa with a fork and allow to cool for 5 to 10 minutes.
5. Remove the quinoa from the pot to a large bowl and toss together with all the salad ingredients until combined. Serve immediately.

Carrot and Pineapple Oatmeal (Pressure Cook)

Prep time: 10 minutes | Cook time: 10 minutes | Serves 8

- 4½ cups water
- 2 cups shredded carrots
- 1 cup steel-cut oats
- 1 (20-ounce / 567-g) can crushed pineapple, undrained
- 1 cup raisins
- 2 teaspoons ground cinnamon
- 1 teaspoon pumpkin pie spice
- Cooking spray
- Brown sugar (optional)

1. Spritz the bottom of the Instant Pot with cooking spray. Place the water, carrots, oats, raisins, pineapple, cinnamon, and pumpkin pie spice into the Instant Pot and stir to combine.
2. Secure the lid. Select the Pressure Cook and set the cooking time for 10 minutes at High Pressure.
3. Once cooking is complete, do a natural pressure release for 10 minutes, then release any remaining pressure. Carefully open the lid.
4. Let the oatmeal stand for 5 to 10 minutes. Sprinkle with the brown sugar, if desired. Serve warm.

Cheesy Chicken and Spinach Breakfast (Pressure Cook)

Prep time: 5 minutes | Cook time: 10 minutes | Serves 4

- 2 tablespoons coconut oil
- 1 pound (454 g) ground chicken
- 1 cup shredded full-fat Cheddar cheese
- 2 tablespoons sugar-free or low-sugar salsa
- ½ cup chopped spinach
- 1 teaspoon curry powder
- ½ teaspoon dried basil
- ½ teaspoon dried parsley
- ½ teaspoon dried cilantro
- 1 tablespoon hot sauce
- ½ teaspoon kosher salt
- ½ teaspoon freshly ground black pepper
- 1 cup filtered water

1. Press the Sauté button on the Instant Pot and heat the coconut oil.
2. Fold in the ground chicken, cheese, salsa, spinach, curry powder, basil, parsley, cilantro, hot sauce, salt, and pepper and stir thoroughly.
3. Pour in the water. Secure the lid. Select the Pressure Cook and set the cooking time for 10 minutes at High Pressure.
4. Once cooking is complete, do a quick pressure release. Carefully open the lid.
5. Serve warm.

Cinnamon Apple Butter (Pressure Cook)

Prep time: 15 minutes | Cook time: 3 minutes | Makes 5 cups

- 4 pounds (1.8 kg) large apples, cored and quartered
- ¾ to 1 cup sugar
- ¼ cup water
- 3 teaspoons ground cinnamon
- ¼ teaspoon ground cloves
- ¼ teaspoon ground allspice
- ¼ teaspoon ground nutmeg
- ¼ cup creamy peanut butter

1. Combine all the ingredients except the butter in the Instant Pot.
2. Secure the lid. Select the Pressure Cook and set the cooking time for 3 minutes at High Pressure.
3. Once cooking is complete, do a natural pressure release for 5 minutes, then release any remaining pressure. Carefully open the lid.
4. Blend the mixture with an immersion blender. Add the peanut butter and whisk until smooth.
5. Let the mixture cool to room temperature. Serve immediately.

Avocado and Bacon Breakfast Burger (Pressure Cook)

Prep time: 5 minutes | Cook time: 10 minutes | Serves 2

- 2 tablespoons coconut oil
- 2 eggs, lightly beaten
- 3 slices no-sugar-added bacon
- ½ cup shredded full-fat Cheddar cheese
- ½ teaspoon kosher salt
- ½ teaspoon freshly ground black pepper
- 1 cup shredded lettuce
- 1 avocado, halved and pitted
- 2 tablespoons sesame seeds

1. Press the Sauté button on the Instant Pot and melt the coconut oil.
2. Fold in the beaten eggs, bacon, cheese, salt, and pepper and stir thoroughly and continuously.
3. When cooked, remove the egg mixture from the pot to a bowl.
4. Assemble the burger: Place an avocado half on a clean work surface and top with the egg mixture and shredded lettuce, and finish with the other half of the avocado. Scatter the sesame seeds on top and serve immediately.

Pumpkin and Pecan Porridge (Pressure Cook)

Prep time: 5 minutes | Cook time: 10 minutes | Serves 2 to 4

- ❀ ¼ cup unsweetened coconut flakes
- ❀ 2 cups filtered water
- ❀ 2 cups full-fat coconut milk
- ❀ 1 cup organic pumpkin purée
- ❀ 1 cup pecans, chopped
- ❀ ¼ cup organic coconut flour
- ❀ ½ teaspoon ground cinnamon
- ❀ ½ teaspoon ginger, finely grated
- ❀ Swerve, to taste (optional)

1. Press the Sauté button on your Instant Pot and toast the coconut flakes, stirring occasionally. Pour in the filtered water and milk.
2. Secure the lid. Press the Pressure Cook on the Instant Pot and set the cooking time for 0 minutes at High Pressure.
3. Once cooking is complete, use a natural pressure release for about 10 minutes and then release any remaining pressure. Carefully remove the lid.
4. Fold in the pumpkin, pecans, flour, cinnamon, ginger, and Swerve (if desired). Let stand for 2 to 4 minutes until desired consistency, stirring occasionally.
5. Ladle the porridge into bowls and serve warm.

Protein-Packed Scrambled Eggs (Pressure Cook)

Prep time: 5 minutes | Cook time: 20 minutes | Serves 2

- ❀ 4 eggs
- ❀ 2 tablespoons coconut oil, plus more for greasing the pot
- ❀ 1 cup filtered water
- ❀ 4 slices no-sugar-added bacon, cooked and finely cut
- ❀ 1 cup spinach, chopped
- ❀ ½ cup shredded full-fat Cheddar cheese
- ❀ ¼ cup full-fat coconut milk
- ❀ ½ teaspoon chili powder
- ❀ ½ teaspoon dried parsley
- ❀ ½ teaspoon dried basil
- ❀ ½ teaspoon ground cumin
- ❀ ½ teaspoon kosher salt
- ❀ ½ teaspoon freshly ground black pepper

1. Grease the inner pot of your Instant Pot. Add all the ingredients. and stir until well mixed.
2. Add the filtered water to the pot.
3. Secure the lid. Press the Pressure Cook on your Instant Pot and set the cooking time for 20 minutes at High Pressure.
4. Once cooking is complete, use a natural pressure release for about 10 minutes and then release any remaining pressure. Carefully remove the lid.
5. Transfer to a serving dish and serve.

Western Omelet (Pressure Cook)

Prep time: 5 minutes | Cook time: 20 minutes | Serves 2

* 2 tablespoons avocado oil
* ¼ cup red bell pepper, finely chopped
* ¼ cup green bell pepper, finely chopped
* ¼ cup onion, chopped
* 6 eggs
* ½ cup shredded full-fat Cheddar cheese
* 2 slices no-sugar-added bacon,

* cooked and finely cut (optional)
* ½ teaspoon dried parsley
* ½ teaspoon dried basil
* ½ teaspoon kosher salt
* ½ teaspoon crushed red pepper
* ½ teaspoon freshly ground black pepper
* Cooking spray
* 1 cup filtered water

1. Press the Sauté button on your Instant Pot. Add and heat the oil. Add the bell pepper and onion and sauté for 4 minutes.
2. Mix together the eggs, cheese, bacon (if desired), parsley, basil, salt, and pepper in a medium bowl and stir well.
3. Spray a glass dish with cooking spray and pour in the mixture. Fold in the sautéed bell pepper and onion, scraping the bits from the pot, and mix well.
4. Add 1 cup of filtered water to the inner pot of the Instant Pot and then place the trivet in the bottom of the pot. Carefully lower the dish into the Instant Pot with a sling.
5. Secure the lid. Press the Pressure Cook on the Instant Pot and set the cooking time for 20 minutes at High Pressure.
6. When the timer beeps, use a natural pressure release for about 10 minutes and then release any remaining pressure. Carefully open the lid.
7. Remove the dish and serve.

Glazed Strawberry Toast (Air Fryer)

Prep time: 5 minutes | Cook time: 8 minutes | Makes 4 toasts

* 4 slices bread, ½-inch thick
* 1 cup sliced strawberries

* 1 teaspoon sugar
* Cooking spray

1. Preheat the air fryer to 375ºF (191ºC).
2. On a clean work surface, lay the bread slices and spritz one side of each slice of bread with cooking spray.
3. Place the bread slices in the air fryer basket, sprayed side down. Top with the strawberries and a sprinkle of sugar.
4. Air fry for 8 minutes until the toast is well browned on each side.
5. Remove from the air fryer basket to a plate and serve.

Air Fryer Baked Eggs

Prep time: 5 minutes | Cook time: 6 minutes | Serves 2

- 2 large eggs
- 2 tablespoons half-and-half
- 2 teaspoons shredded Cheddar cheese
- Salt and freshly ground black pepper, to taste
- Cooking spray

1. Preheat the air fryer to 330ºF (166ºC).
2. Spritz 2 ramekins lightly with cooking spray. Crack an egg into each ramekin.
3. Top each egg with 1 tablespoon of half-and-half and 1 teaspoon of Cheddar cheese. Sprinkle with salt and black pepper. Stir the egg mixture with a fork until well combined.
4. Place the ramekins in the air fryer basket and bake for 6 minutes until set. Check for doneness and cook for 1 minute as needed.
5. Allow to cool for 5 minutes in the basket before removing and serving.

Maple Walnut Pancake (Air Fryer)

Prep time: 10 minutes | Cook time: 20 minutes | Serves 4

- 3 tablespoons melted butter, divided
- 1 cup flour
- 2 tablespoons sugar
- 1½ teaspoons baking powder
- ¼ teaspoon salt
- 1 egg, beaten
- ¾ cup milk
- 1 teaspoon pure vanilla extract
- ½ cup roughly chopped walnuts
- Maple syrup or fresh sliced fruit, for serving

1. Preheat the air fryer to 330ºF (166ºC). Grease a baking pan with 1 tablespoon of melted butter.
2. Mix together the flour, sugar, baking powder, and salt in a medium bowl. Add the beaten egg, milk, the remaining 2 tablespoons of melted butter, and vanilla and stir until the batter is sticky but slightly lumpy.
3. Slowly pour the batter into the greased baking pan and scatter with the walnuts.
4. Place the pan in the air fryer basket and bake for 20 minutes until golden brown and cooked through.
5. Let the pancake rest for 5 minutes and serve topped with the maple syrup or fresh fruit, if desired.

Peppered Maple Bacon Knots (Air Fryer)

Prep time: 5 minutes | Cook time: 7 to 8 minutes | Serves 6

* 1 pound (454 g) maple smoked center-cut bacon
* ¼ cup maple syrup
* ¼ cup brown sugar
* Coarsely cracked black peppercorns, to taste

1. Preheat the air fryer to 390ºF (199ºC).
2. On a clean work surface, tie each bacon strip in a loose knot.
3. Stir together the maple syrup and brown sugar in a bowl. Generously brush this mixture over the bacon knots.
4. Working in batches, arrange the bacon knots in the air fryer basket. Sprinkle with the coarsely cracked black peppercorns.
5. Air fry for 5 minutes. Flip the bacon knots and continue cooking for 2 to 3 minutes more, or until the bacon is crisp.
6. Remove from the basket to a paper towel-lined plate. Repeat with the remaining bacon knots.
7. Let the bacon knots cool for a few minutes and serve warm.

Cinnamon Sweet Potato Chips (Air Fryer)

Prep time: 5 minutes | Cook time: 8 minutes | Makes 6 to 8 slices

* 1 small sweet potato, cut into ⅜ inch-thick slices
* 2 tablespoons olive oil
* 1 to 2 teaspoon ground cinnamon

1. Preheat the air fryer to 390ºF (199ºC).
2. Add the sweet potato slices and olive oil in a bowl and toss to coat. Fold in the cinnamon and stir to combine.
3. Arrange the sweet potato slices in a single layer in the air fryer basket.
4. Air fry for 8 minutes, or until the chips are crisp. Shake the basket halfway through.
5. Remove from the air fryer basket and allow to cool for 5 minutes before serving.

Ham and Cheese Toast (Air Fryer)

Prep time: 5 minutes | Cook time: 6 minutes | Serves: 1

- 1 slice bread
- 1 teaspoon butter, at room temperature
- 1 egg
- Salt and freshly ground black

- pepper, to taste
- 2 teaspoons diced ham
- 1 tablespoon grated Cheddar cheese

1. Preheat the air fryer to 325ºF (163ºC).
2. On a clean work surface, use a 2½-inch biscuit cutter to make a hole in the center of the bread slice with about ½-inch of bread remaining.
3. Spread the butter on both sides of the bread slice. Crack the egg into the hole and season with salt and pepper to taste.
4. Transfer the bread to the air fryer basket. Air fry for 5 minutes. Scatter the cheese and diced ham on top and continue to cook for an additional 1 minute until the egg is set and the cheese has melted.
5. Remove the toast from the basket to a plate and let cool for 5 minutes before serving.

Herbed Cheddar Frittata (Air Fryer)

Prep time: 10 minutes | Cook time: 20 minutes | Serves 4

- ½ cup shredded Cheddar cheese
- ½ cup half-and-half
- 4 large eggs
- 2 tablespoons chopped scallion greens

- 2 tablespoons chopped fresh parsley
- ½ teaspoon kosher salt
- ½ teaspoon ground black pepper
- Cooking spray

1. Preheat the air fryer to 300ºF (149ºC). Spritz a baking pan with cooking spray.
2. Whisk together all the ingredients in a large bowl, then pour the mixture into the prepared baking pan.
3. Set the pan in the preheated air fryer and bake for 20 minutes or until set.
4. Serve immediately.

Kale Frittata (Air Fryer)

Prep time: 5 minutes | Cook time: 11 minutes | Serves 2

- 1 cup kale, chopped
- 1 teaspoon olive oil
- 4 large eggs, beaten
- Kosher salt, to taste
- 2 tablespoons water
- 3 tablespoons crumbled feta
- Cooking spray

1. Preheat the air fryer to 360ºF (182ºC). Spritz an air fryer baking pan with cooking spray.
2. Add the kale to the baking pan and drizzle with olive oil. Arrange the pan in the preheated air fryer. Broil for 3 minutes.
3. Meanwhile, combine the eggs with salt and water in a large bowl. Stir to mix well.
4. Make the frittata: When the broiling time is complete, pour the eggs into the baking pan and spread with feta cheese. Reduce the temperature to 300ºF (149ºC).
5. Bake for 8 minutes or until the eggs are set and the cheese melts.
6. Remove the baking pan from the air fryer and serve the frittata immediately.

Sausage and Cheese Quiche (Air Fryer)

Prep time: 5 minutes | Cook time: 25 minutes | Serves 4

- 12 large eggs
- 1 cup heavy cream
- Salt and black pepper, to taste
- 12 ounces (340 g) sugar-free
- breakfast sausage
- 2 cups shredded Cheddar cheese
- Cooking spray

1. Preheat the air fryer to 375ºF (191ºC). Coat a casserole dish with cooking spray.
2. Beat together the eggs, heavy cream, salt and pepper in a large bowl until creamy. Stir in the breakfast sausage and Cheddar cheese.
3. Pour the sausage mixture into the prepared casserole dish and bake for 25 minutes, or until the top of the quiche is golden brown and the eggs are set.
4. Remove from the air fryer and let sit for 5 to 10 minutes before serving.

Mixed Berry Dutch Baby Pancake (Air Fryer)

Prep time: 10 minutes | Cook time: 12 to 16 minutes | Serves 4

- 1 tablespoon unsalted butter, at room temperature
- 1 egg
- 2 egg whites
- ½ cup 2% milk
- ½ cup whole-wheat pastry flour
- 1 teaspoon pure vanilla extract
- 1 cup sliced fresh strawberries
- ½ cup fresh raspberries
- ½ cup fresh blueberries

1. Preheat the air fryer to 330ºF (166ºC). Grease a baking pan with the butter.
2. Using a hand mixer, beat together the egg, egg whites, milk, pastry flour, and vanilla in a medium mixing bowl until well incorporated.
3. Pour the batter into the pan and bake in the preheated air fryer for 12 to 16 minutes, or until the pancake puffs up in the center and the edges are golden brown.
4. Allow the pancake to cool for 5 minutes and serve topped with the berries.

Bacon and Egg Bread Cups (Air Fryer)

Prep time: 10 minutes | Cook time: 8 to 12 minutes | Serves 4

- 4 (3-by-4-inch) crusty rolls
- 4 thin slices Gouda or Swiss cheese mini wedges
- 5 eggs
- 2 tablespoons heavy cream
- 3 strips precooked bacon, chopped
- ½ teaspoon dried thyme
- Pinch salt
- Freshly ground black pepper, to taste

1. Preheat the air fryer to 330ºF (166ºC).
2. On a clean work surface, cut the tops off the rolls. Using your fingers, remove the insides of the rolls to make bread cups, leaving a ½-inch shell. Place a slice of cheese onto each roll bottom.
3. Whisk together the eggs and heavy cream in a medium bowl until well combined. Fold in the bacon, thyme, salt, and pepper and stir well.
4. Scrape the egg mixture into the prepared bread cups.
5. Transfer the bread cups to the basket and bake for 8 to 12 minutes, or until the eggs are cooked to your preference.
6. Serve warm.

Chapter 3 Vegetables

Gold Potato and Boiled Egg Salad (Pressure Cook)

Prep time: 20 minutes | Cook time: 12 minutes | Serves 4

* 1 cup water
* 1 pound (454 g) small Yukon Gold potatoes
* 2 boiled eggs, peeled and chopped
* 1 celery rib, diced
* ¼ cup pickle relish
* ½ yellow onion, sliced
* 1 garlic clove, minced
* ⅓ cup mayonnaise
* ½ teaspoon fresh rosemary, chopped
* ½ tablespoon yellow mustard
* ⅓ teaspoon cayenne pepper
* Sea salt and ground black pepper, to taste

1. Pour the water in the Instant Pot and fit in a steamer basket. Place the potatoes in the steamer basket.
2. Secure the lid. Choose the Pressure Cook and set the cooking time for 12 minutes at High pressure.
3. Once cooking is complete, do a quick pressure release. Carefully remove the lid. Allow to cool for a few minutes until cool enough to handle.
4. Peel and slice the potatoes, then place them in a large bowl and toss with the remaining ingredients. Stir to combine.
5. Serve immediately.

Squash and Carrot Curry with Tofu (Pressure Cook)

Prep time: 10 minutes | Cook time: 12 minutes | Serves 4

* 1 tablespoon canola oil
* 1 large onion, sliced
* 4 cubes (about 2⅝ ounces / 74 g in total) mild Japanese curry sauce mix
* 1½ cups water
* 1 pound (454 g) winter squash, peeled and cut into 1-inch chunks
* 2 large carrots, peeled and cut into 1-inch-thick slices
* 1 pound (454 g) extra-firm tofu, cut into 1-inch cubes

1. Select the Sauté mode of the Instant Pot. Heat the canola oil until shimmering.
2. Add the onions and sauté for 4 minutes or until translucent.
3. Add the curry mix and water in the pot. Break up the curry cubes with a wooden spoon.
4. Add the squash and carrots and stir to combine. Arrange the tofu cubes on top.
5. Lock the lid. Select the Manual function, and set the cooking time for 8 minutes at High Pressure.
6. When the cooking time is up, quick release the pressure. Carefully open the lid. Stir gently to combine the tofu and other ingredients. Serve immediately.

Mediterranean Herbed Cabbage (Pressure Cook)

Prep time: 10 minutes | Cook time: 6 minutes | Serves 4

- 1 (1-pound / 454-g) head cabbage, cut into wedges
- 1 bell pepper, chopped
- 1 carrot, chopped
- 1 bay leaf
- 1 sprig thyme
- 1 sprig rosemary
- 1 cup roasted vegetable broth
- ½ teaspoon cayenne pepper
- 2 tablespoons olive oil
- Sea salt and ground black pepper, to taste

1. Add all ingredients to the Instant Pot. Stir to combine.
2. Secure the lid. Choose the Pressure Cook and set the cooking time for 6 minutes at High pressure.
3. Once cooking is complete, perform a quick pressure release. Carefully open the lid. Discard the bay leaf, thyme, and rosemary.
4. Divide them into bowls and serve warm.

Vegetable Basmati Rice (Pressure Cook)

Prep time: 10 minutes | Cook time: 9 to 10 minutes | Serves 6 to 8

- 3 tablespoons olive oil
- 3 cloves garlic, minced
- 1 large onion, finely chopped
- 3 tablespoons chopped cilantro stalks
- 1 cup garden peas, frozen
- 1 cup sweet corn, frozen
- 2 cups basmati rice, rinsed
- 1 teaspoon turmeric powder
- ¼ teaspoon salt
- 3 cups chicken stock
- 2 tablespoons butter (optional)

1. Press the Sauté button on the Instant Pot and heat the olive oil.
2. Add the garlic, onion, and cilantro and sauté for 5 to 6 minutes, stirring occasionally, or until the garlic is fragrant.
3. Stir in the peas, sweet corn, and rice. Scatter with the turmeric and salt. Pour in the chicken stock and stir to combine.
4. Lock the lid. Select the Pressure Cook and set the cooking time for 4 minutes at High Pressure.
5. Once cooking is complete, do a quick pressure release. Carefully open the lid.
6. You can add the butter, if desired. Serve warm.

Basmati Rice (Pressure Cook)

Prep time: 5 minutes | Cook time: 6 minutes | Serves 4

- 1 cup white basmati rice, rinsed
- 1¼ cups water
- ¼ teaspoon salt
- Butter to taste (optional)

1. Combine all the ingredients except the butter in the Instant Pot.
2. Lock the lid. Select the Pressure Cook and set the cooking time for 6 minutes at High Pressure.
3. Once cooking is complete, do a natural pressure release for 10 minutes, then release any remaining pressure. Carefully remove the lid.
4. Fluff the rice with a fork. You can stir in the butter, if desired. Serve warm.

Chipotle Styled Rice (Pressure Cook)

Prep time: 10 minutes | Cook time: 30 minutes | Serves 4 to 6

- 2 cups brown rice, rinsed
- 2¾ cups water
- 4 small bay leaves
- 1 lime, juiced
- 1½ tablespoons olive oil
- 1 teaspoon salt
- ½ cup chopped cilantro

1. Place the rice, water, and bay leaves into the Instant Pot and stir.
2. Lock the lid. Select the Rice mode and set the cooking time for 30 minutes at High Pressure.
3. When the timer beeps, perform a natural pressure release for 10 minutes, then release any remaining pressure. Carefully remove the lid.
4. Add the lime juice, olive oil, salt, and cilantro and stir to mix well. Serve immediately.

Steamed Lemony Cabbage (Pressure Cook)

Prep time: 10 minutes | Cook time: 2 minutes | Serves 2 to 4

- 1 cup water
- 1 large cabbage, cut into wedges
- Juice of 1 lemon
- 2 tablespoons melted butter
- Salt and black pepper, to taste
- ¼ teaspoon red chili flakes

1. Pour the water in the Instant Pot, then fit in a trivet. Place the cabbage in the trivet.
2. Seal the lid. Select the Pressure Cook and set the time for 2 minutes at High Pressure.
3. Once cooking is complete, do a quick pressure release, then unlock the lid. Transfer the cabbage on a plate.
4. In a bowl, whisk together the lemon juice, butter, salt, pepper, and chili flakes.
5. Drizzle the mixture all over the cabbage and serve.

Broccoli, Spinach, and Avocado Mash (Pressure Cook)

Prep time: 15 minutes | Cook time: 3 minutes | Serves 4

* 1 medium broccoli, cut into florets
* 2 cups spinach
* 1 cup vegetable broth
* 2 avocados, halved, pitted, and peeled
* 2 tablespoons chopped parsley

* 2 tablespoons butter
* Salt and black pepper, to taste
* 3 tablespoons Greek yogurt
* 2 tablespoons toasted pine nuts, for topping

1. Add the broccoli, spinach, and broth to the Instant Pot. Stir to mix well.
2. Seal the lid. Select the Pressure Cook and set the cooking time for 3 minutes at High Pressure.
3. Once cooking is complete, do a quick pressure release. Carefully open the lid. Stir in the avocado, parsley, butter, salt, pepper, and Greek yogurt.
4. Pour the mixture in a food processor and pulse until smooth. Spoon into serving bowls and top with pine nuts. Serve immediately.

Rice Bowl with Raisins and Almonds (Pressure Cook)

Prep time: 5 minutes | Cook time: 20 minutes | Serves 4

* 1 cup brown rice
* 1 cup water
* 1 cup coconut milk
* ½ cup coconut chips
* ½ cup maple syrup

* ¼ cup raisins
* ¼ cup almonds
* A pinch of cinnamon powder
* Salt, to taste

1. Place the rice and water into the Instant Pot and give a stir.
2. Secure the lid. Select the Pressure Cook and set the cooking time for 15 minutes at High Pressure.
3. When the timer beeps, perform a quick pressure release. Carefully remove the lid.
4. Stir in the coconut milk, coconut chips, maple syrup, raisins, almonds, cinnamon powder, and salt.
5. Lock the lid. Select the Pressure Cook and set the cooking time for 5 minutes at High Pressure.
6. Once cooking is complete, do a quick pressure release. Open the lid.
7. Serve warm.

Onion-Artichoke Corn Risotto (Pressure Cook)

Prep time: 15 minutes | Cook time: 13 minutes | Serves 4

- ❀ 2 tablespoons olive oil
- ❀ 2 large white onions, chopped
- ❀ 1 medium zucchini, chopped
- ❀ 4 garlic cloves, minced
- ❀ Salt and black pepper, to taste
- ❀ 1 cup Arborio rice
- ❀ ½ cup white wine
- ❀ 2½ cups chicken stock
- ❀ 2 cups corn kernels
- ❀ 1 (6-ounce / 170-g) can artichokes, drained and chopped
- ❀ 1 cup grated Parmesan cheese
- ❀ 3 tablespoons lemon juice
- ❀ 1 tablespoon lemon zest
- ❀ ¼ cup chopped basil, plus more for garnish

1. Set the Instant Pot on the Sauté function and heat the olive oil. Add the onions, zucchini and garlic to the pot and sauté for 5 minutes, or until tender. Season with salt and pepper. Stir in the rice and cook for 2 minutes, or until translucent.
2. Pour in the white wine and keep cooking until it has a thick consistency and reduces about one-third. Stir in the chicken stock, corn, salt and pepper.
3. Lock the lid. Select the Pressure Cook and set the cooking time for 6 minutes at High Pressure. When the timer goes off, use a natural pressure release for 15 minutes, then release any remaining pressure. Carefully open the lid.
4. Add the artichokes, cheese, lemon juice and zest and whisk until risotto is sticky. Stir in the chopped basil and transfer the risotto into bowls. Serve garnished with the basil.

Cheesy Asparagus (Pressure Cook)

Prep time: 10 minutes | Cook time: 8 minutes | Serves 4

- ❀ 1 cup water
- ❀ 1 pound (454 g) asparagus, chopped
- ❀ 2 garlic cloves, minced
- ❀ 2 tablespoons butter, softened
- ❀ Salt and black pepper, to taste
- ❀ 1 tablespoon olive oil
- ❀ ½ lemon, juiced
- ❀ 2 tablespoons grated Parmesan cheese

1. In the Instant pot, pour the water and fit in a trivet. Cut out a foil sheet, place the asparagus on top with garlic and butter. Season with salt and black pepper. Wrap the foil and place on the trivet.
2. Seal the lid. Select the Pressure Cook and set to 8 minutes at High Pressure.
3. Once cooking is complete, do a quick pressure release. Carefully open the lid.
4. Remove the foil, then transfer the asparagus onto a platter. Drizzle with lemon juice, and top with Parmesan cheese to serve.

Scalloped Potatoes (Air Fryer)

Prep time: 5 minutes | Cook time: 20 minutes | Serves 4

- 2 cup sliced frozen potatoes, thawed
- 3 cloves garlic, minced
- Pinch salt
- Freshly ground black pepper, to taste
- ¾ cup heavy cream

1. Preheat the air fryer to 380ºF (193ºC).
2. Toss the potatoes with the garlic, salt, and black pepper in a baking pan until evenly coated. Pour the heavy cream over the top.
3. Place the baking pan in the air fryer basket and bake for 15 minutes, or until the potatoes are tender and top is golden brown. Check for doneness and bake for another 5 minutes as needed.
4. Serve hot.

Cinnamon-Spiced Acorn Squash (Air Fryer)

Prep time: 5 minutes | Cook time: 15 minutes | Serves 2

- 1 medium acorn squash, halved crosswise and deseeded
- 1 teaspoon coconut oil
- 1 teaspoon light brown sugar
- Few dashes of ground cinnamon
- Few dashes of ground nutmeg

1. Preheat the air fryer to 325ºF (163ºC).
2. On a clean work surface, rub the cut sides of the acorn squash with coconut oil. Scatter with the brown sugar, cinnamon, and nutmeg.
3. Put the squash halves in the air fryer basket, cut-side up. Air fry for 15 minutes until just tender when pierced in the center with a paring knife.
4. Rest for 5 to 10 minutes and serve warm.

Bok Choy with Rice Wine Vinegar (Pressure Cook)

Prep time: 5 minutes | Cook time: 6 minutes | Serves 4

- 1 teaspoon sesame oil
- 1 clove garlic, pressed
- 1 pound (454 g) Bok choy
- ½ cup water
- 1 tablespoon rice wine vinegar
- 2 tablespoons soy sauce

1. Press the Sauté button and heat the sesame oil in the Instant Pot.
2. Add the garlic and sauté for 1 minute or until fragrant. Add the Bok choy and pour in the water.
3. Secure the lid. Choose the Pressure Cook and set the cooking time for 5 minutes at High pressure.
4. Meanwhile, in a small bowl, whisk the rice vinegar and soy sauce.
5. Once cooking is complete, do a quick pressure release. Carefully open the lid.
6. Drizzle the sauce over the Bok choy and serve immediately.

Cauliflower and Celeriac Mix (Pressure Cook)

Prep time: 10 minutes | Cook time: 2 minutes | Serves 4

* 1 cup water
* 1 head cauliflower, cut into florets
* 1 carrot, sliced
* ½ cup celeriac, sliced
* 2 tablespoons butter
* Salt and black pepper, to taste

1. Pour the water into the Instant Pot and fit in a steamer basket. Place the cauliflower, carrots, and celeriac in the basket.
2. Seal the lid. Select the Steam mode, then set the cooking time for 2 minutes at High Pressure.
3. Once cooking time is complete, perform a quick pressure release. Unlock the lid and transfer the veggies to a bowl.
4. Stir in the butter and sprinkle with salt and pepper before serving.

Charred Green Beans with Sesame Seeds (Air Fryer)

Prep time: 5 minutes | Cook time: 8 minutes | Serves 4

* 1 tablespoon reduced-sodium soy sauce or tamari
* ½ tablespoon Sriracha sauce
* 4 teaspoons toasted sesame oil, divided
* 12 ounces (340 g) trimmed green beans
* ½ tablespoon toasted sesame seeds

1. Preheat the air fryer to 375ºF (191ºC).
2. Whisk together the soy sauce, Sriracha sauce, and 1 teaspoon of sesame oil in a small bowl until smooth.
3. Toss the green beans with the remaining sesame oil in a large bowl until evenly coated.
4. Place the green beans in the air fryer basket in a single layer. You may need to work in batches to avoid overcrowding.
5. Air fry for about 8 minutes until the green beans are lightly charred and tender. Shake the basket halfway through the cooking time.
6. Remove from the basket to a platter. Repeat with the remaining green beans.
7. Pour the prepared sauce over the top of green beans and toss well. Serve sprinkled with the toasted sesame seeds.

Vegetable Pasta (Pressure Cook)

Prep time: 10 minutes | Cook time: 7 minutes | Serves 4 to 6

- ✿ 2 cups dried pasta
- ✿ 1 cup water
- ✿ ½ jar spaghetti sauce
- ✿ ½ can chickpeas, rinsed and drained
- ✿ ½ can black olives, rinsed and drained

- ✿ ½ cup frozen spinach
- ✿ ½ cup frozen lima beans
- ✿ ½ squash, shredded
- ✿ ½ zucchini, sliced
- ✿ ½ tablespoon Italian seasoning
- ✿ ½ teaspoon cumin
- ✿ ½ teaspoon garlic powder

1. Add all the ingredients to the Instant Pot and stir to combine.
2. Press the Pressure Cook on the Instant Pot and set the cooking time for 7 minutes at High Pressure.
3. Once cooking is complete, perform a natural pressure release for 10 minutes and then release any remaining pressure. Carefully open the lid.
4. Transfer to a serving dish and serve immediately.

Bulgur Wheat Bowl with Shallots (Pressure Cook)

Prep time: 5 minutes | Cook time: 14 minutes | Serves 2

- ✿ 1 tablespoon butter
- ✿ 2 shallots, chopped
- ✿ 1 teaspoon minced fresh garlic
- ✿ 1 cup vegetable broth

- ✿ ½ cup bulgur wheat
- ✿ ¼ teaspoon sea salt
- ✿ ¼ teaspoon ground black pepper

1. Set the Instant Pot to the Sauté mode and melt the butter. Add the shallots to the pot and sauté for 3 minutes, or until just tender and fragrant. Add the garlic and sauté for 1 minute, or until fragrant. Stir together the remaining ingredients in the pot.
2. Lock the lid. Select the Pressure Cook and set the cooking time for 10 minutes at High Pressure. When the timer beeps, perform a natural pressure release for 10 minutes, then release any remaining pressure. Carefully open the lid.
3. Fluff the bulgur wheat with a fork and serve immediately.

Braised Pinto Beans with Pancetta (Pressure Cook)

Prep time: 10 minutes | Cook time: 45 minutes | Serves 6

- 4 ounces (113 g) pancetta, chopped
- 1 tablespoon olive oil
- 1 onion, finely chopped
- 1 garlic clove, minced
- 1 pound (454 g) dried pinto beans,
- soaked
- 4 cups water
- ½ teaspoon ground cumin
- Salt and black pepper, to taste
- 3 tablespoons chopped parsley

1. Set the Instant Pot to the Sauté mode and heat the olive oil. Add the pancetta, onion and garlic to the pot and sauté for 5 minutes. Whisk in the beans, water, cumin, salt and pepper.
2. Lock the lid. Select the Pressure Cook and set the cooking time for 40 minutes at High Pressure. When the timer beeps, perform a natural pressure release for 10 minutes, then release any remaining pressure. Carefully open the lid.
3. Serve topped with the chopped parsley.

Cannellini Beans with Bacon (Pressure Cook)

Prep time: 5 minutes | Cook time: 14 minutes | Serves 4

- 3 bacon slices, chopped
- 2 (15-ounce / 425-g) cans cannel in beans, rinsed and drained
- 1 cup water
- ½ cup canned tomatoes
- 1 tablespoon ground mustard
- 1 teaspoon chili powder
- 1 cup cooked white rice
- ¼ cup chopped mint

1. Set the Instant Pot on the Sauté mode. Add the bacon to the pot and cook for 6 minutes, or until crispy and browned. Transfer the bacon to a plate with paper towels to soak up excess fat.
2. Add the cannellini beans, water, tomatoes, mustard and chili powder to the pot. Place the bacon back in the pot.
3. Lock the lid. Select the Pressure Cook and set the cooking time for 8 minutes at High Pressure. When the timer goes off, use a natural pressure release for 10 minutes, then release any remaining pressure. Carefully open the lid.
4. Stir in the cooked white rice and serve garnished with the chopped mint.

Cheesy Black Beans (Pressure Cook)

Prep time: 10 minutes | Cook time: 15 minutes | Serves 2

- 🌸 1 teaspoon olive oil
- 🌸 1 large white onion, chopped
- 🌸 1 teaspoon grated garlic
- 🌸 3 cups vegetable broth
- 🌸 1 cup dried black beans, soaked

- 🌸 1 teaspoon Mexican seasoning
- 🌸 Salt, to taste
- 🌸 ½ cup Cotija cheese
- 🌸 ¼ cup chopped cilantro

1. Set the Instant Pot to the Sauté mode and heat the olive oil. Add the onion and garlic to the pot and sauté for 3 minutes, or until tender. Stir in the vegetable broth, black beans, Mexican seasoning and salt.
2. Set the lid in place. Select the Pressure Cook and set the cooking time for 12 minutes at High Pressure. When the timer goes off, perform a quick pressure release. Carefully open the lid.
3. Divide the beans between 2 plates and serve topped with the Cotija cheese and cilantro.

Panko Green Beans (Air Fryer)

Prep time: 5 minutes | Cook time: 15 minutes | Serves 4

- 🌸 ½ cup flour
- 🌸 2 eggs
- 🌸 1 cup panko bread crumbs
- 🌸 ½ cup grated Parmesan cheese

- 🌸 1 teaspoon cayenne pepper
- 🌸 Salt and black pepper, to taste
- 🌸 1½ pounds (680 g) green beans

1. Preheat the air fryer to 400ºF (204ºC).
2. In a bowl, place the flour. In a separate bowl, lightly beat the eggs. In a separate shallow bowl, thoroughly combine the bread crumbs, cheese, cayenne pepper, salt, and pepper.
3. Dip the green beans in the flour, then in the beaten eggs, finally in the bread crumb mixture to coat well.
4. Place the green beans in the air fryer basket and air fry for 15 minutes, shaking the basket halfway through, or until they are cooked to your desired crispiness.
5. Remove from the basket to a bowl and serve.

Air Fryer Veggies with Halloumi

Prep time: 5 minutes | Cook time: 14 minutes | Serves 2

* 2 zucchinis, cut into even chunks
* 1 large eggplant, peeled, cut into chunks
* 1 large carrot, cut into chunks
* 6 ounces (170 g) halloumi cheese,
* cubed
* 2 teaspoons olive oil
* Salt and black pepper, to taste
* 1 teaspoon dried mixed herbs

1. Preheat the air fryer to 340ºF (171ºC).
2. Combine the zucchinis, eggplant, carrot, cheese, olive oil, salt, and pepper in a large bowl and toss to coat well.
3. Spread the mixture evenly in the air fryer basket and air fry for 14 minutes until crispy and golden, shaking the basket once during cooking.
4. Serve topped with mixed herbs.

Easy Cheesy Vegetable Quesadilla (Air Fryer)

Prep time: 5 minutes | Cook time: 10 minutes | Serves 1

* 1 teaspoon olive oil
* 2 flour tortillas
* ¼ zucchini, sliced
* ¼ yellow bell pepper, sliced
* ¼ cup shredded gouda cheese
* 1 tablespoon chopped cilantro
* ½ green onion, sliced

1. Preheat the air fryer to 390ºF (199ºC). Coat the air fryer basket with 1 teaspoon of olive oil.
2. Arrange a flour tortilla in the air fryer basket and scatter the top with zucchini, bell pepper, gouda cheese, cilantro, and green onion. Place the other flour tortilla on top.
3. Air fry for 10 minutes until the tortillas are lightly browned and the vegetables are tender.
4. Remove from the basket and cool for 5 minutes before slicing into wedges.

Crispy Tofu Sticks (Air Fryer)

Prep time: 5 minutes | Cook time: 14 minutes | Serves 4

- 2 tablespoons olive oil, divided
- ½ cup flour
- ½ cup crushed cornflakes
- Salt and black pepper, to taste
- 14 ounces (397 g) firm tofu, cut into ½-inch-thick strips

1. Preheat the air fryer to 360ºF (182ºC). Grease the air fryer basket with 1 tablespoon of olive oil.
2. Combine the flour, cornflakes, salt, and pepper on a plate.
3. Dredge the tofu strips in the flour mixture until they are completely coated. Transfer the tofu strips to the greased air fryer basket.
4. Brush the remaining 1 tablespoon of olive oil over the top of tofu strips. Air fry for 14 minutes until crispy, flipping the tofu strips halfway through.
5. Serve warm.

Teriyaki Cauliflower (Air Fryer)

Prep time: 5 minutes | Cook time: 14 minutes | Serves 4

- ½ cup soy sauce
- ⅓ cup water
- 1 tablespoon brown sugar
- 1 teaspoon sesame oil
- 1 teaspoon cornstarch
- 2 cloves garlic, chopped
- ½ teaspoon chili powder
- 1 big cauliflower head, cut into florets

1. Preheat the air fryer to 340ºF (171ºC).
2. Make the teriyaki sauce: In a small bowl, whisk together the soy sauce, water, brown sugar, sesame oil, cornstarch, garlic, and chili powder until well combined.
3. Place the cauliflower florets in a large bowl and drizzle the top with the prepared teriyaki sauce and toss to coat well.
4. Put the cauliflower florets in the air fryer basket and air fry for 14 minutes, shaking the basket halfway through, or until the cauliflower is crisp-tender.
5. Let the cauliflower cool for 5 minutes before serving.

Cheesy Cabbage Wedges (Air Fryer)

Prep time: 5 minutes | Cook time: 20 minutes | Serves 4

❀ 4 tablespoons melted butter
❀ 1 head cabbage, cut into wedges
❀ 1 cup shredded Parmesan cheese
❀ Salt and black pepper, to taste
❀ ½ cup shredded Mozzarella cheese

1. Preheat the air fryer to 380ºF (193ºC).
2. Brush the melted butter over the cut sides of cabbage wedges and sprinkle both sides with the Parmesan cheese. Season with salt and pepper to taste.
3. Place the cabbage wedges in the air fryer basket and air fry for 20 minutes, flipping the cabbage halfway through, or until the cabbage wedges are lightly browned.
4. Transfer the cabbage wedges to a plate and serve with the Mozzarella cheese sprinkled on top.

Rosemary Roasted Squash with Cheese (Air Fryer)

Prep time: 5 minutes | Cook time: 20 minutes | Serves 2

❀ 1 pound (454 g) butternut squash, cut into wedges
❀ 2 tablespoons olive oil
❀ 1 tablespoon dried rosemary
❀ Salt, to salt
❀ 1 cup crumbled goat cheese
❀ 1 tablespoon maple syrup

1. Preheat the air fryer to 350ºF (177ºC).
2. Toss the squash wedges with the olive oil, rosemary, and salt in a large bowl until well coated.
3. Transfer the squash wedges to the air fryer basket, spreading them out in as even a layer as possible.
4. Roast for 10 minutes. Flip the squash and roast for another 10 minutes until golden brown.
5. Sprinkle the goat cheese on top and serve drizzled with the maple syrup.

Parmesan Zucchini Chips (Air Fryer)

Prep time: 5 minutes | Cook time: 14 minutes | Serves 4

- 2 egg whites
- Salt and black pepper, to taste
- ½ cup seasoned bread crumbs
- 2 tablespoons grated Parmesan
- cheese
- ¼ teaspoon garlic powder
- 2 medium zucchinis, sliced
- Cooking spray

1. Preheat the air fryer to 400ºF (204ºC). Spritz the air fryer basket with cooking spray.
2. In a bowl, beat the egg whites with salt and pepper. In a separate bowl, thoroughly combine the bread crumbs, Parmesan cheese, and garlic powder.
3. Dredge the zucchini slices in the egg white, then coat in the bread crumb mixture.
4. Arrange the zucchini slices in the air fryer basket and air fry for 14 minutes, flipping the zucchini halfway through.
5. Remove from the basket to a plate and serve.

Stuffed Portobello Mushrooms with Vegetables (Air Fryer)

Prep time: 5 minutes | Cook time: 8 to 12 minutes | Serves 4

- 4 portobello mushrooms, stem removed
- 1 tablespoon olive oil
- 1 tomato, diced
- ½ green bell pepper, diced
- ½ small red onion, diced
- ½ teaspoon garlic powder
- Salt and black pepper, to taste
- ½ cup grated Mozzarella cheese

1. Preheat the air fryer to 330ºF (166ºC).
2. Using a spoon to scoop out the gills of the mushrooms and discard them. Brush the mushrooms with the olive oil.
3. In a mixing bowl, stir together the remaining ingredients except the Mozzarella cheese. Using a spoon to stuff each mushroom with the filling and scatter the Mozzarella cheese on top.
4. Arrange the mushrooms in the air fryer basket and roast for 8 to 12 minutes, or until the cheese is melted.
5. Serve warm.

Cheese-Walnut Stuffed Mushrooms (Air Fryer)

Prep time: 5 minutes | Cook time: 10 minutes | Serves 4

* 4 large portobello mushrooms
* 1 tablespoon canola oil
* ½ cup shredded Mozzarella cheese
* ⅓ cup minced walnuts
* 2 tablespoons chopped fresh parsley
* Cooking spray

1. Preheat the air fryer to 350ºF (177ºC). Spritz the air fryer basket with cooking spray.
2. On a clean work surface, remove the mushroom stems. Scoop out the gills with a spoon and discard. Coat the mushrooms with canola oil. Top each mushroom evenly with the shredded Mozzarella cheese, followed by the minced walnuts.
3. Arrange the mushrooms in the air fryer and roast for 10 minutes until golden brown.
4. Transfer the mushrooms to a plate and sprinkle the parsley on top for garnish before serving.

Creamy Corn Casserole (Air Fryer)

Prep time: 5 minutes | Cook time: 15 minutes | Serves 4

* 2 cups frozen yellow corn
* 1 egg, beaten
* 3 tablespoons flour
* ½ cup grated Swiss or Havarti cheese
* ½ cup light cream
* ¼ cup milk
* Pinch salt
* Freshly ground black pepper, to taste
* 2 tablespoons butter, cut into cubes
* Nonstick cooking spray

1. Preheat the air fryer to 320ºF (160ºC). Spritz a baking pan with nonstick cooking spray.
2. Stir together the remaining ingredients except the butter in a medium bowl until well incorporated.
3. Transfer the mixture to the prepared baking pan and scatter with the butter cubes.
4. Place the baking pan in the air fryer basket and bake for 15 minutes, or until the top is golden brown and a toothpick inserted in the center comes out clean.
5. Let the casserole cool for 5 minutes before slicing into wedges and serving.

Chapter 4 Soup and Stew

Carrot and Cabbage Beef Stew (Pressure Cook)

Prep time: 10 minutes | Cook time: 19 minutes | Serves 4 to 6

- 3 tablespoons extra-virgin olive oil
- 2 large carrots, peeled and sliced into ¼-inch disks and then quartered
- 1 large Spanish onion, diced
- 2 pounds (907 g) ground beef
- 3 cloves garlic, minced
- 1 (46-ounce / 1.3-kg) can tomato juice
- 2 cups vegetable broth
- Juice of 2 lemons
- 1 head cabbage, cored and roughly chopped
- ½ cup jasmine rice
- ¼ cup dark brown sugar
- 1 tablespoon Worcestershire sauce
- 2 teaspoons seasoned salt
- 1 teaspoon black pepper
- 3 bay leaves

1. Set the Instant Pot to the Sauté mode and heat the oil for 3 minutes. Add the carrots and onion to the pot and sauté for 3 minutes, or until just tender. Add the ground beef and garlic to the pot and sauté for 3 minutes, or until the beef is lightly browned. Stir in the remaining ingredients.
2. Lock the lid. Select the Pressure Cook and set the cooking time for 10 minutes at High Pressure. When the timer goes off, perform a quick pressure release. Carefully open the lid.
3. Let rest for 5 minutes to thicken and cool before serving.

Chicken Soup with Egg Noodles (Pressure Cook)

Prep time: 15 minutes | Cook time: 24 minutes | Serves 8

- 1 (3½-pound / 1.5-kg) chicken, cut into pieces
- 4 cups low-sodium chicken broth
- 3 stalks celery, chopped
- 2 medium carrots, peeled and chopped
- 1 medium yellow onion, peeled and chopped
- 1 clove garlic, and smashed
- 1 bay leaf
- 1 teaspoon poultry seasoning
- ½ teaspoon dried thyme
- 1 teaspoon salt
- ¼ teaspoon ground black pepper
- 4 ounces (113 g) dried egg noodles

1. Add all the ingredients, except for the egg noodles, to the Instant Pot and stir to combine.
2. Set the lid in place. Select the Soup mode and set the cooking time for 20 minutes at High Pressure. Once cooking is complete, use a natural pressure release for 20 to 25 minutes, then release any remaining pressure. Carefully open the lid.
3. Remove and discard the bay leaf. Transfer the chicken to a clean work surface. Shred chicken and discard the skin and bones. Return the shredded chicken to the pot and stir to combine. Stir in the noodles.
4. Lock the lid. Select the Pressure Cook and set the cooking time for 4 minutes at High Pressure. Once cooking is complete, use a quick pressure release. Carefully open the lid.
5. Serve hot.

Cheesy Veggie Orzo Soup (Pressure Cook)

Prep time: 15 minutes | Cook time: 10 minutes | Serves 4

* 1 medium potato, peeled and small-diced
* 1 medium zucchini, diced
* 1 small carrot, peeled and diced
* 1 small yellow onion, peeled and diced
* 2 stalks celery, diced
* 1 (15-ounce / 425-g) can diced tomatoes, undrained
* 2 cloves garlic, peeled and minced
* ½ cup gluten-free orzo
* 5 cups vegetable broth
* 2 teaspoons dried oregano leaves
* 2 teaspoons dried thyme leaves
* 1 teaspoon salt
* 1 teaspoon ground black pepper
* 3 cups fresh baby spinach
* 4 tablespoons grated Parmesan cheese

1. Add all the ingredients, except for the spinach and Parmesan cheese, to the Instant Pot.
2. Lock the lid. Select the Manual setting and set the cooking time for 10 minutes at High Pressure. Once the timer goes off, use a quick pressure release. Carefully open the lid.
3. Stir in the spinach until wilted.
4. Ladle the soup into four bowls and garnish with the Parmesan cheese. Serve warm.

Coconut Red Bean Soup (Pressure Cook)

Prep time: 10 minutes | Cook time: 50 minutes | Serves 4

* 2 teaspoons olive oil
* 3 slices bacon, diced
* 2 large carrots, peeled and diced
* 5 green onions, sliced
* 1 stalk celery, chopped
* 1 Scotch bonnet, deseeded, veins removed and minced
* 1 (15-ounce / 425-g) can diced tomatoes, undrained
* ½ pound (227 g) dried small red beans
* 1 (13.5-ounce / 383-g) can coconut milk
* 2 cups chicken broth
* 1 tablespoon Jamaican jerk seasoning
* 1 teaspoon salt
* 4 cups cooked basmati rice
* 1 cup chopped fresh parsley
* 1 lime, quartered

1. Press the Sauté button on the Instant Pot and heat the oil. Add the bacon, carrots, onions, celery and Scotch bonnet to the pot and sauté for 5 minutes, or until the onions are translucent.
2. Stir in the tomatoes with juice, red beans, coconut milk, chicken broth, Jamaican jerk seasoning and salt.
3. Lock the lid. Select the Pressure Cook and set the cooking time for 45 minutes at High Pressure. When the timer goes off, do a natural pressure release for 10 minutes, then release any remaining pressure. Carefully open the lid.
4. Ladle the soup into four bowls over cooked rice and garnish with parsley. Squeeze a quarter of lime over each bowl. Serve warm.

Chinese Pork Belly Stew (Pressure Cook)

Prep time: 10 minutes | Cook time: 42 minutes | Serves 8

- ½ cup plus 2 tablespoons soy sauce, divided
- ¼ cup Chinese cooking wine
- ½ cup packed light brown sugar
- 2 pounds (907 g) pork belly, skinned and cubed
- 12 scallions, cut into pieces
- 3 cloves garlic, minced
- 3 tablespoons vegetable oil
- 1 teaspoon Chinese five-spice powder
- 2 cups vegetable broth
- 4 cups cooked white rice

1. In a large bowl, whisk together ½ cup of the soy sauce, wine and brown sugar. Place the pork into the bowl and turn to coat evenly. Cover in plastic and refrigerate for at least 4 hours. Drain the pork and pat dry. Reserve the marinade.
2. Press the Sauté button on the Instant Pot and heat the oil. Add half the pork to the pot in an even layer, making sure there is space between pork cubes to prevent steam from forming. Sear the pork for 3 minutes on each side, or until lightly browned. Transfer the browned pork to a plate. Repeat with the remaining pork.
3. Stir in the remaining ingredients, except for the rice. Return the browned pork to the pot with the reserved marinade.
4. Lock the lid. Select the Pressure Cook and set the cooking time for 30 minutes at High Pressure. When the timer beeps, perform a natural pressure release for 20 minutes, then release any remaining pressure. Carefully open the lid.
5. Serve hot over cooked rice.

Potato Bisque with Bacon (Pressure Cook)

Prep time: 10 minutes | Cook time: 20 minutes | Serves 4

- 2 tablespoons unsalted butter
- 1 slice bacon, diced
- 3 leeks, trimmed, rinsed and diced
- 6 cups diced Yukon Gold potatoes
- 4 cups chicken broth
- 2 teaspoons dried thyme leaves
- 1 teaspoon sriracha
- ½ teaspoon sea salt
- ¼ cup whole milk

1. Set the Instant Pot on the Sauté mode and melt the butter. Add the bacon and leeks to the pot and sauté for 5 minutes, or until the fat is rendered and leeks become tender.
2. Stir in the remaining ingredients, except for the milk.
3. Lock the lid. Select the Pressure Cook and set the cooking time for 15 minutes at High Pressure. When the timer goes off, use a natural pressure release for 5 minutes, then release any remaining pressure. Carefully open the lid.
4. Pour the milk into the pot. Use an immersion blender to blend the soup in the pot until it achieves the desired consistency.
5. Ladle the bisque into 4 bowls and serve warm.

Chuck Roast with Onions (Pressure Cook)

Prep time: 20 minutes | Cook time: 1 hour 2 minutes | Serves 6

- 2½ pounds (1.1 kg) boneless chuck roast, cut into pieces
- 1 teaspoon salt
- 1 teaspoon ground black pepper
- 1 tablespoon olive oil
- 2 medium yellow onions, peeled and chopped
- 2 medium red bell peppers, deseeded and chopped
- 6 cloves garlic, peeled and minced
- 2 teaspoons ground cumin
- 2 teaspoons dried oregano
- 2 teaspoons smoked paprika
- ½ teaspoon cayenne pepper
- ½ cup white wine
- 1 (14.5-ounce / 411-g) can diced tomatoes
- 1 bay leaf
- ½ cup halved Spanish olives
- 2 teaspoons distilled white vinegar

1. Season the chuck roast with the salt and pepper on all sides. Set aside.
2. Press the Sauté button on the Instant Pot and heat the oil. Add half the seasoned meat to the pot and sear for 7 minutes on both sides, or until well browned. Transfer the browned meat to a platter and set aside. Repeat with the remaining meat.
3. Add the onions and bell peppers to the pot and sauté for 5 minutes, or until just softened. Add the garlic, cumin, oregano, paprika and cayenne pepper to the pot and sauté for 1 minute, or until fragrant.
4. Pour in the white wine and cook for 2 minutes, or until the liquid is reduced by half. Return the browned meat back to the pot along with the tomatoes and bay leaf.
5. Close and secure the lid. Select the Manual setting and set the cooking time for 40 minutes at High Pressure. Once the timer goes off, use a quick pressure release. Carefully open the lid.
6. Remove and discard the bay leaf. Stir in the olives and vinegar. Serve hot.

Potato and Fish Stew (Pressure Cook)

Prep time: 15 minutes | Cook time: 28 minutes | Serves 8

- ❀ 2 tablespoons unsalted butter
- ❀ 2 stalks celery, chopped
- ❀ 1 medium carrot, peeled and diced
- ❀ 1 medium yellow onion, peeled and diced
- ❀ 2 cloves garlic, peeled and minced
- ❀ 1 teaspoon Italian seasoning
- ❀ ¼ teaspoon dried thyme
- ❀ ¼ teaspoon salt
- ❀ ¼ teaspoon ground black pepper
- ❀ 1 cup lager-style beer
- ❀ 1 (28-ounce / 794-g) can diced tomatoes
- ❀ 2 large Russet potatoes, peeled and diced
- ❀ 3 cups seafood stock
- ❀ 1 bay leaf
- ❀ 2 pounds (907 g) cod, cut into pieces
- ❀ 2 tablespoons lemon juice

1. Set the Instant Pot to the Sauté mode and melt the butter. Add the celery, carrot and onion to the pot and sauté for 8 minutes, or until softened. Add the garlic, Italian seasoning, thyme, salt and pepper to the pot and cook for 30 seconds.
2. Pour in the beer and scrape the bottom of the pot well. Stir in the tomatoes, potatoes, seafood stock and bay leaf.
3. Set the lid in place. Select the Pressure Cook and set the cooking time for 10 minutes at High Pressure. When the timer goes off, perform a quick pressure release. Carefully open the lid.
4. Stir in the fish. Select the Sauté mode and allow the soup to simmer for 10 minutes, or until the fish is cooked through. Remove and discard the bay leaf and stir in lemon juice. Serve hot.

Beef Chili with Onions (Pressure Cook)

Prep time: 20 minutes | Cook time: 19 minutes | Serves 8

- 2 pounds (907 g) 90% lean ground beef
- 3 large yellow onions, peeled and diced, divided
- 3 cloves garlic, peeled and minced
- 2 (16-ounce / 454-g) cans kidney beans, rinsed and drained
- 1 (15-ounce / 425-g) can tomato sauce
- 1 cup beef broth
- 2 tablespoons semisweet chocolate chips
- 2 tablespoons honey
- 2 tablespoons red wine vinegar
- 2 tablespoons chili powder
- 1 tablespoon pumpkin pie spice
- 1 teaspoon ground cumin
- ½ teaspoon ground cardamom
- ½ teaspoon salt
- ½ teaspoon freshly cracked black pepper
- ¼ teaspoon ground cloves
- 1 pound (454 g) cooked spaghetti
- 4 cups shredded Cheddar cheese

1. Press the Sauté button on the Instant Pot. Add the ground beef and ¾ of the diced onions to the pot and sauté for 8 minutes, or until the beef is browned and the onions are transparent. Drain the beef mixture and discard any excess fat. Add the garlic to the pot and sauté for 30 seconds.
2. Stir in the remaining ingredients, except for the reserved onions, spaghetti and cheese. Cook for 1 minute, or until fragrant.
3. Set the lid in place. Select the Pressure Cook and set the cooking time for 10 minutes at High Pressure. When the timer goes off, perform a quick pressure release. Carefully open the lid.
4. Serve over the cooked spaghetti and top with the reserved onions and cheese.

Pork Meatball Soup (Pressure Cook)

Prep time: 15 minutes | Cook time: 19 minutes | Serves 4

Meatballs:
- ½ pound (227 g) ground pork
- 2 tablespoons gluten-free bread crumbs
- 2 tablespoons grated Parmesan cheese
- 1 tablespoon Italian seasoning
- ½ teaspoon cayenne pepper
- ½ teaspoon salt
- 1 large egg, whisked
- 2 cloves garlic, peeled and minced
- 2 tablespoons olive oil, divided

Soup:
- 1 tablespoon olive oil
- 1 medium carrot, peeled and shredded
- 1 Russet potato, scrubbed and small-diced
- 1 small red onion, peeled and diced
- 1 (15-ounce / 425-g) can diced
- fire-roasted tomatoes, undrained
- 4 cups beef broth
- ½ teaspoon salt
- ½ teaspoon ground black pepper
- ½ teaspoon red pepper flakes
- ½ cup chopped fresh basil leaves

1. In a medium bowl, stir together all the ingredients for the meatballs, except for the olive oil. Shape the mixture into 24 meatballs.
2. Set the Instant Pot to the Sauté mode and heat 1 tablespoon of the olive oil for 30 seconds. Add half the meatballs to the pot and sear for 3 minutes, turning them to brown all sides. Remove the first batch and set aside. Add the remaining 1 tablespoon of the olive oil to the pot and repeat with the remaining meatballs. Remove the meatballs from the pot.
3. Select the Sauté mode and heat the olive oil for 30 seconds. Add the carrot, potato and onion to the pot and sauté for 5 minutes, or until the onion becomes translucent.
4. Add the meatballs to the pot along with the remaining ingredients for the soup.
5. Close and secure the lid. Select the Pressure Cook and set the cooking time for 7 minutes at High Pressure. Once cooking is complete, use a quick pressure release. Carefully open the lid.
6. Serve warm.

Peppery Chicken Chili (Pressure Cook)

Prep time: 15 minutes | Cook time: 36 minutes | Serves 8

- 2 tablespoons unsalted butter
- 1 medium yellow onion, peeled and chopped
- ½ pound (227 g) Anaheim peppers, deseeded and roughly chopped
- ½ pound (227 g) poblano peppers, deseeded and roughly chopped
- ½ pound (227 g) tomatillos, husked and quartered
- 2 small jalapeño peppers, deseeded and roughly chopped
- 2 cloves garlic, peeled and minced
- 1 teaspoon ground cumin
- 6 bone-in, skin-on chicken thighs (2½ pounds / 1.1 kg total)
- 2 cups chicken stock
- 2 cups water
- ⅓ cup roughly chopped fresh cilantro
- 3 (15-ounce / 425-g) cans Great Northern beans, drained and rinsed

1. Press the Sauté button on the Instant Pot and melt the butter. Add the onion and sauté for 3 minutes, or until tender. Add Anaheim peppers, poblano peppers, tomatillos and jalapeño peppers to the pot and sauté for 3 minutes.
2. Add the garlic and cumin to the pot and sauté for 30 seconds, or until fragrant. Stir in the chicken thighs, stock and water.
3. Lock the lid. Select the Bean/Chili mode and set the cooking time for 30 minutes at High Pressure. When the timer goes off, perform a quick pressure release. Carefully open the lid.
4. Transfer the chicken thighs to a clean work surface. Use two forks to remove the skin off the chicken and shred the meat.
5. Use an immersion blender to purée the mixture in the pot until smooth. Stir in the shredded chicken, cilantro and beans. Serve warm.

Veggie Corn Chowder (Pressure Cook)

Prep time: 20 minutes | Cook time: 25 to 28 minutes | Serves 8

- ❀ 6 slices bacon, divided
- ❀ 1 large carrot, peeled and diced
- ❀ 1 large sweet onion, peeled and diced
- ❀ ½ cup diced celery
- ❀ 2 large Yukon Gold potatoes, peeled and diced
- ❀ 6 cups chicken broth

- ❀ 3 cups fresh corn kernels
- ❀ 2 tablespoons fresh thyme leaves, divided
- ❀ 1 teaspoon sea salt
- ❀ 1 teaspoon ground black pepper
- ❀ ½ teaspoon honey
- ❀ 1 bay leaf
- ❀ 1 cup heavy cream

1. Set the Instant Pot to the Sauté mode. Add the bacon to the pot and sear for 5 minutes, or until crispy. Transfer the bacon to a plate lined with paper towels and set aside.
2. Add the carrot, onion and celery to the pot and sauté for 3 to 5 minutes, or until the onion is translucent. Add the potatoes to the pot and continue to sauté for 2 to 3 minutes, or until the potatoes are lightly browned.
3. Stir in the chicken broth, corn, 1 tablespoon of the thyme, salt, pepper, honey and bay leaf. Crumble 2 pieces of the bacon and add to the soup.
4. Set the lid in place. Select the Pressure Cook and set the cooking time for 15 minutes at High Pressure. When the timer goes off, perform a quick pressure release. Carefully open the lid.
5. Remove and discard the bay leaf. Whisk int the heavy cream and use an immersion blender to purée the soup in the pot.
6. Divide the soup among bowls and garnish with the remaining 1 tablespoon of the thyme leaves. Crumble 4 pieces of the bacon and add to the soup.
7. Serve warm.

Chapter 5 Poultry

Lemony Chicken With Potatoes (Pressure Cook)

Prep time: 5 minutes | Cook time: 21 minutes | Serves 4

- 2 pounds (907 g) chicken thighs
- 1 teaspoon fine sea salt
- ½ teaspoon ground black pepper
- 2 tablespoons olive oil
- ¼ cup freshly squeezed lemon juice
- ¾ cup low-sodium chicken broth
- 2 tablespoons Italian seasoning
- 2 to 3 tablespoons Dijon mustard
- 2 to 3 pounds (907 to 1361 g) red potatoes, quartered

1. Sprinkle the chicken with the salt and pepper.
2. Add the oil to your Instant Pot. Select the Sauté mode. Add the chicken and sauté for 3 minutes until browned on both sides.
3. Meanwhile, make the sauce by stirring together the lemon juice, chicken broth, Italian seasoning, and mustard in a medium mixing bowl.
4. Drizzle the sauce over the chicken. Fold in the potatoes.
5. Secure the lid. Press the Pressure Cook on the Instant Pot and cook for 15 minutes at High Pressure.
6. Once cooking is complete, do a quick pressure release. Carefully remove the lid.
7. Transfer the chicken to a serving dish and serve immediately.

Paprika Chicken with Cucumber Salad (Pressure Cook)

Prep time: 10 minutes | Cook time: 20 minutes | Serves 4

- 1 tablespoon olive oil
- 1 yellow onion, chopped
- 2 chicken breasts, skinless, boneless and halved
- 1 cup chicken stock
- 1 tablespoon sweet paprika
- ½ teaspoon cinnamon powder

Salad:

- 2 cucumbers, sliced
- 1 tomato, cubed
- 1 avocado, peeled, pitted, and
- cubed
- 1 tablespoon chopped cilantro

1. Press the Sauté button on the Instant Pot and heat the olive oil until it shimmers.
2. Add the onion and chicken breasts and sauté for 5 minutes, stirring occasionally, or until the onion is translucent. Stir in the chicken stock, paprika, and cinnamon powder.
3. Secure the lid. Select the Pressure Cook and set the cooking time for 15 minutes at High Pressure.
4. Meanwhile, toss all the ingredients for the salad in a bowl. Set aside.
5. Once cooking is complete, do a natural pressure release for 10 minutes, then release any remaining pressure. Carefully open the lid.
6. Divide the chicken breasts between four plates and serve with the salad on the side.

Keto Bruschetta Chicken (Pressure Cook)

Prep time: 5 minutes | Cook time: 20 minutes | Serves 2

* ½ cup filtered water
* 2 boneless, skinless chicken breasts
* 1 (14-ounce / 397-g) can sugar-free or low-sugar crushed tomatoes
* ¼ teaspoon dried basil
* ½ cup shredded full-fat Cheddar cheese
* ¼ cup heavy whipping cream

1. Add the filtered water, chicken breasts, tomatoes, and basil to your Instant Pot.
2. Lock the lid. Press the Pressure Cook and set the cooking time for 20 minutes at High Pressure.
3. Once cooking is complete, use a quick pressure release. Carefully open the lid.
4. Fold in the cheese and cream and stir until the cheese is melted.
5. Serve immediately.

Rosemary Turkey Breast (Air Fryer)

Prep time: 2 hours 20 minutes | Cook time: 30 minutes | Serves 6

* ½ teaspoon dried rosemary
* 2 minced garlic cloves
* 2 teaspoons salt
* 1 teaspoon ground black pepper
* ¼ cup olive oil
* 2½ pounds (1.1 kg) turkey breast
* ¼ cup pure maple syrup
* 1 tablespoon stone-ground brown mustard
* 1 tablespoon melted vegan butter

1. Combine the rosemary, garlic, salt, ground black pepper, and olive oil in a large bowl. Stir to mix well.
2. Dunk the turkey breast in the mixture and wrap the bowl in plastic. Refrigerate for 2 hours to marinate.
3. Remove the bowl from the refrigerator and let sit for half an hour before cooking.
4. Preheat the air fryer to 400ºF (204ºC). Spritz the air fryer basket with cooking spray.
5. Remove the turkey from the marinade and place in the preheated air fry and air fry for 20 minutes or until well browned. Flip the breast halfway through.
6. Meanwhile, combine the remaining ingredients in a small bowl. Stir to mix well.
7. Pour half of the butter mixture over the turkey breast in the air fryer and air fry for 10 more minutes. Flip the breast and pour the remaining half of butter mixture over halfway through.
8. Transfer the turkey on a plate and slice to serve.

Easy Chicken Fingers (Air Fryer)

Prep time: 20 minutes | Cook time: 30 minutes | Makes 12 chicken fingers

- ½ cup all-purpose flour
- 2 cups panko bread crumbs
- 2 tablespoons canola oil
- 1 large egg
- 3 boneless and skinless chicken
- breasts, each cut into 4 strips
- Kosher salt and freshly ground black pepper, to taste
- Cooking spray

1. Preheat the air fryer to 360°F (182°C). Spritz the air fryer basket with cooking spray.
2. Pour the flour in a large bowl. Combine the panko and canola oil on a shallow dish. Whisk the egg in a separate bowl.
3. Rub the chicken strips with salt and ground black pepper on a clean work surface, then dip the chicken in the bowl of flour. Shake the excess off and dunk the chicken strips in the bowl of whisked egg, then roll the strips over the panko to coat well.
4. Arrange 4 strips in the air fryer basket each time and air fry for 10 minutes or until crunchy and lightly browned. Flip the strips halfway through. Repeat with remaining ingredients.
5. Serve immediately.

Crack Chicken with Bacon (Pressure Cook)

Prep time: 5 minutes | Cook time: 15 minutes | Serves 2

- ½ cup grass-fed bone broth
- ½ pound (227 g) boneless, skinless chicken breasts
- 2 ounces (57 g) cream cheese, softened
- ¼ cup tablespoons keto-friendly
- ranch dressing
- 3 slices bacon, cooked, chopped into small pieces
- ½ cup shredded full-fat Cheddar cheese

1. Add the bone broth, chicken, cream cheese, and ranch dressing to your Instant Pot and stir to combine.
2. Secure the lid. Press the Pressure Cook and set the cooking time for 15 minutes at High Pressure.
3. When the timer goes off, do a quick pressure release. Carefully open the lid.
4. Add the bacon and cheese and stir until the cheese has melted.
5. Serve.

Sweet and Sour Chicken (Pressure Cook)

Prep time: 5 minutes | Cook time: 20 minutes | Serves 8

- 1 tablespoon olive oil
- 4 cloves garlic, minced
- 1 onion, chopped
- 2 pounds (907 g) chicken meat
- 1 green bell pepper, julienned

- ½ cup molasses
- ½ cup ketchup
- ¼ cup soy sauce
- 1 tablespoon cornstarch, mixed with 2 tablespoons water

1. Set your Instant Pot to Sauté and heat the olive oil.
2. Add the garlic, onion, and chicken and stir-fry for about 5 minutes until lightly golden.
3. Stir in the bell pepper, molasses, ketchup, and soy sauce.
4. Secure the lid. Select the Poultry mode and set the cooking time for 15 minutes at High Pressure.
5. Once cooking is complete, do a quick pressure release. Carefully open the lid.
6. Set your Instant Pot to Sauté again and whisk in the cornstarch mixture until thickened.
7. Allow to cool for 5 minutes before serving.

Citrusy Chicken Tacos (Pressure Cook)

Prep time: 5 minutes | Cook time: 20 minutes | Serves 12

- ¼ cup olive oil
- 12 chicken breasts, skin and bones removed
- 8 cloves of garlic, minced
- ⅔ cup orange juice, freshly squeezed

- ⅔ cup lime juice, freshly squeezed
- 2 tablespoons ground cumin
- 1 tablespoon dried oregano
- 1 tablespoon orange peel
- Salt and pepper, to taste
- ¼ cup cilantro, chopped

1. Set your Instant Pot to Sauté. Add and heat the oil.
2. Add the chicken breasts and garlic. Cook until the chicken pieces are lightly browned.
3. Add the orange juice, lime juice, cumin, oregano, orange peel, salt, and pepper. Stir well.
4. Secure the lid. Select the Poultry mode and cook for 15 minutes at High Pressure.
5. Once cooking is complete, do a quick pressure release. Carefully remove the lid.
6. Serve garnished with the cilantro.

Chili Chicken Zoodles (Pressure Cook)

Prep time: 10 minutes | Cook time: 20 minutes | Serves 4

* 2 chicken breasts, skinless, boneless and halved
* 1½ cups chicken stock
* 3 celery stalks, chopped
* 1 tablespoon tomato sauce
* 1 teaspoon chili powder
* A pinch of salt and black pepper
* 2 zucchinis, spiralized
* 1 tablespoon chopped cilantro

1. Mix together all the ingredients except the zucchini noodles and cilantro in the Instant Pot.
2. Secure the lid. Select the Pressure Cook and set the cooking time for 15 minutes at High Pressure.
3. Once cooking is complete, do a natural pressure release for 10 minutes, then release any remaining pressure. Carefully open the lid.
4. Set your Instant Pot to Sauté and add the zucchini noodles. Cook for about 5 minutes, stirring often, or until softened.
5. Sprinkle the cilantro on top for garnish before serving.

Apricot-Glazed Chicken Drumsticks (Air Fryer)

Prep time: 15 minutes | Cook time: 30 minutes | Makes 6 drumsticks

For the Glaze:
* ½ cup apricot preserves
* ½ teaspoon tamari
* ¼ teaspoon chili powder
* 2 teaspoons Dijon mustard

For the Chicken:
* 6 chicken drumsticks
* ½ teaspoon seasoning salt
* 1 teaspoon salt
* ½ teaspoon ground black pepper
* Cooking spray

Make the glaze:
1. Combine the ingredients for the glaze in a saucepan, then heat over low heat for 10 minutes or until thickened.
2. Turn off the heat and sit until ready to use.

Make the Chicken:
1. Preheat the air fryer to 370ºF (188ºC). Spritz the air fryer basket with cooking spray.
2. Combine the seasoning salt, salt, and pepper in a small bowl. Stir to mix well.
3. Place the chicken drumsticks in the preheated air fryer. Spritz with cooking spray and sprinkle with the salt mixture on both sides.
4. Air fry for 20 minutes or until well browned. Flip the chicken halfway through.
5. Baste the chicken with the glaze and air fryer for 2 more minutes or until the chicken tenderloin is glossy.
6. Serve immediately.

Garlic Chicken (Pressure Cook)

Prep time: 10 minutes | Cook time: 20 minutes | Serves 4

* 2 chicken breasts, skinless, boneless and halved
* 1 cup tomato sauce
* ¼ cup sweet chili sauce
* ¼ cup chicken stock
* 4 garlic cloves, minced
* 1 tablespoon chopped basil

1. Combine all the ingredients in the Instant Pot.
2. Secure the lid. Select the Poultry mode and set the cooking time for 20 minutes at High Pressure.
3. Once cooking is complete, do a natural pressure release for 10 minutes, then release any remaining pressure. Carefully open the lid.
4. Divide the chicken breasts among four plates and serve.

Bruschetta Chicken (Air Fryer)

Prep time: 10 minutes | Cook time: 20 minutes | Serves 4

Bruschetta Stuffing:
* 1 tomato, diced
* 3 tablespoons balsamic vinegar
* 1 teaspoon Italian seasoning
* 2 tablespoons chopped fresh basil
* 3 garlic cloves, minced
* 2 tablespoons extra-virgin olive oil

Chicken:
* 4 (4-ounce / 113-g) boneless, skinless chicken breasts, cut 4 slits each
* 1 teaspoon Italian seasoning
* Chicken seasoning or rub, to taste
* Cooking spray

1. Preheat the air fryer to 370ºF (188ºC). Spritz the air fryer basket with cooking spray.
2. Combine the ingredients for the bruschetta stuffing in a bowl. Stir to mix well. Set aside.
3. Rub the chicken breasts with Italian seasoning and chicken seasoning on a clean work surface.
4. Arrange the chicken breasts, slits side up, in a single layer in the air fryer basket and spritz with cooking spray. You may need to work in batches to avoid overcrowding.
5. Air fry for 7 minutes, then open the air fryer and fill the slits in the chicken with the bruschetta stuffing. Cook for another 3 minutes or until the chicken is well browned.
6. Serve immediately.

Simple Chicken Nuggets (Air Fryer)

Prep time: 10 minutes | Cook time: 20 minutes | Serves 4

- 1 pound (454 g) boneless, skinless chicken breasts, cut into 1-inch pieces
- 2 tablespoons panko bread crumbs
- 6 tablespoons bread crumbs
- Chicken seasoning or rub, to taste
- Salt and ground black pepper, to taste
- 2 eggs
- Cooking spray

1. Preheat the air fryer to 400°F (204°C). Spritz the air fryer basket with cooking spray.
2. Combine the bread crumbs, chicken seasoning, salt, and black pepper in a large bowl. Stir to mix well. Whisk the eggs in a separate bowl.
3. Dunk the chicken pieces in the egg mixture, then in the breadcrumb mixture. Shake the excess off.
4. Arrange the well-coated chicken pieces in the preheated air fryer. Spritz with cooking spray and air fry for 8 minutes or until crispy and golden brown. Shake the basket halfway through. You may need to work in batches to avoid overcrowding.
5. Serve immediately.

Simple Air Fried Chicken Wings

Prep time: 10 minutes | Cook time: 15 minutes | Serves 4

- 1 tablespoon olive oil
- 8 whole chicken wings
- Chicken seasoning or rub, to taste
- 1 teaspoon garlic powder
- Freshly ground black pepper, to taste

1. Preheat the air fryer to 400°F (204°C). Grease the air fryer basket with olive oil.
2. On a clean work surface, rub the chicken wings with chicken seasoning and rub, garlic powder, and ground black pepper.
3. Arrange the well-coated chicken wings in the preheated air fryer. Air fry for 15 minutes or until the internal temperature of the chicken wings reaches at least 165°F (74°C). Flip the chicken wings halfway through.
4. Remove the chicken wings from the air fryer. Serve immediately.

Browned Chicken with Veggies (Pressure Cook)

Prep time: 10 minutes | Cook time: 25 minutes | Serves 4

- 2 tablespoons olive oil
- 1 yellow onion, chopped
- 2 chicken breasts, skinless, boneless and cubed
- 1 cup cubed mixed bell peppers
- 1 cup cubed tomato
- 1 cup chicken stock
- 1 teaspoon Creole seasoning
- A pinch of cayenne pepper

1. Set your Instant Pot to Sauté and heat the olive oil until hot.
2. Add the onion and chicken cubes and brown for 5 minutes. Stir in the remaining ingredients.
3. Secure the lid. Select the poultry mode and set the cooking time for 20 minutes at High Pressure.
4. Once cooking is complete, do a natural pressure release for 10 minutes, then release any remaining pressure. Carefully open the lid.
5. Serve warm.

Creamy Chicken with Cilantro (Pressure Cook)

Prep time: 5 minutes | Cook time: 25 minutes | Serves 4

- 2 chicken breasts, skinless, boneless and halved
- 1 cup tomato sauce
- 1 cup plain Greek yogurt
- ¾ cup coconut cream
- ¼ cup chopped cilantro
- 2 teaspoons garam masala
- 2 teaspoons ground cumin
- A pinch of salt and black pepper

1. Thoroughly combine all the ingredients in the Instant Pot.
2. Lock the lid. Select the Poultry mode and set the cooking time for 25 minutes at High Pressure.
3. Once cooking is complete, do a natural pressure release for 5 minutes, then release any remaining pressure. Carefully open the lid.
4. Transfer the chicken breasts to a plate and serve.

Spicy Mexican Chicken (Pressure Cook)

Prep time: 5 minutes | Cook time: 17 minutes | Serves 4

- 2 tablespoons avocado oil
- ½ cup water
- 1 pound (454 g) ground chicken
- 1 (14-ounce / 397-g) can low-sugar fire roasted tomatoes
- ½ jalapeño, finely chopped
- ¼ poblano chili pepper, finely chopped
- ½ teaspoon crushed red pepper
- ½ teaspoon coriander
- ½ teaspoon chili powder
- ½ teaspoon curry powder
- ½ teaspoon kosher salt
- ½ teaspoon freshly ground black pepper

1. Press the Sauté button on the Instant Pot and heat the avocado oil.
2. Pour the water into the Instant Pot and stir in the remaining ingredients.
3. Secure the lid. Select the Pressure Cook and set the cooking time for 17 minutes at High Pressure.
4. Once cooking is complete, do a quick pressure release. Carefully open the lid.
5. Let the chicken cool for 5 minutes and serve.

Instant Pot Whole Chicken (Pressure Cook)

Prep time: 5 minutes | Cook time: 25 minutes | Serves 6

- 4 tablespoons grass-fed butter, softened
- 1 teaspoon dried cilantro
- 1 teaspoon dried basil
- ½ teaspoon kosher salt
- ½ teaspoon freshly ground black pepper
- ½ cup grass-fed bone broth
- 1 whole chicken

1. Stir together the softened butter, cilantro, basil, salt, and pepper in a large bowl until combined.
2. Pour the bone broth into the Instant Pot. Place the chicken in the Instant Pot with the breast facing down and lightly baste with the butter mixture.
3. Secure the lid. Select the Meat/Stew mode and set the cooking time for 25 minutes at High Pressure.
4. Once cooking is complete, do a natural pressure release for 15 minutes, then release any remaining pressure. Carefully open the lid.
5. Remove the chicken from the Instant Pot and serve.

Paprika Chicken (Pressure Cook)

Prep time: 5 minutes | Cook time: 40 minutes | Serves 6

- ❀ 1¾ tablespoons olive oil
- ❀ 1½ teaspoons salt
- ❀ ½ teaspoon pepper
- ❀ 1 teaspoon minced garlic
- ❀ 1 teaspoon paprika
- ❀ 1 whole chicken
- ❀ 1 cup chicken broth

1. Stir together the olive oil, salt, pepper, garlic, and paprika in a small bowl. Rub the mixture all over the chicken until evenly coated.
2. Pour the chicken broth into the Instant Pot and add the coated chicken.
3. Secure the lid. Select the Poultry mode and set the cooking time for 40 minutes at High Pressure.
4. Once cooking is complete, do a natural pressure release for 15 minutes, then release any remaining pressure. Carefully open the lid.
5. Serve warm.

Chicken Cacciatore (Pressure Cook)

Prep time: 15 minutes | Cook time: 15 minutes | Serves 6

- ❀ 1 broiler/fryer chicken (3 to 4 pounds / 1.4 to 1.8 kg), cut up and skin removed
- ❀ 1 (4-ounce / 113-g) can mushroom stems and pieces, drained
- ❀ 1 (14½-ounce / 411-g) can diced tomatoes, undrained
- ❀ 1 (8-ounce / 227-g) can tomato sauce
- ❀ ¼ cup white wine or water
- ❀ 2 medium onions, thinly sliced
- ❀ 2 garlic cloves, minced
- ❀ 1 bay leaf
- ❀ 1 to 2 teaspoon dried oregano
- ❀ ½ teaspoon dried basil
- ❀ 1 teaspoon salt
- ❀ ¼ teaspoon pepper

1. Combine all the ingredients in the Instant Pot.
2. Secure the lid. Select the Poultry mode and set the cooking time for 15 minutes at High Pressure.
3. Once cooking is complete, do a natural pressure release for 10 minutes, then release any remaining pressure. Carefully open the lid.
4. Discard the bay leaf and serve on a plate.

Simple Whole Chicken Bake (Air Fryer)

Prep time: 10 minutes | Cook time: 1 hour | Serves 2 to 4

- ½ cup melted butter
- 3 tablespoons garlic, minced
- Salt, to taste
- 1 teaspoon ground black pepper
- 1 (1-pound / 454-g) whole chicken

1. Preheat the air fryer to 350ºF (177ºC).
2. Combine the butter with garlic, salt, and ground black pepper in a small bowl.
3. Brush the butter mixture over the whole chicken, then place the chicken in the preheated air fryer, skin side down.
4. Bake the chicken for an hour or until an instant-read thermometer inserted in the thickest part of the chicken registers at least 165ºF (74ºC). Flip the chicken halfway through.
5. Remove the chicken from the air fryer and allow to cool for 15 minutes before serving.

Golden Chicken Cutlets (Air Fryer)

Prep time: 15 minutes | Cook time: 15 minutes | Serves 4

- 2 tablespoons panko bread crumbs
- ¼ cup grated Parmesan cheese
- ⅛ tablespoon paprika
- ½ tablespoon garlic powder
- 2 large eggs
- 4 chicken cutlets
- 1 tablespoon parsley
- Salt and ground black pepper, to taste
- Cooking spray

1. Preheat the air fryer to 400ºF (204ºC). Spritz the air fryer basket with cooking spray.
2. Combine the bread crumbs, Parmesan, paprika, garlic powder, salt, and ground black pepper in a large bowl. Stir to mix well. Beat the eggs in a separate bowl.
3. Dredge the chicken cutlets in the beaten eggs, then roll over the bread crumbs mixture to coat well. Shake the excess off.
4. Transfer the chicken cutlets in the preheated air fryer and spritz with cooking spray.
5. Air fry for 15 minutes or until crispy and golden brown. Flip the cutlets halfway through.
6. Serve with parsley on top.

Easy Cajun Chicken Drumsticks (Air Fryer)

Prep time: 5 minutes | Cook time: 40 minutes | Serves 5

* 1 tablespoon olive oil
* 10 chicken drumsticks
* 1½ tablespoons Cajun seasoning
* Salt and ground black pepper, to taste

1. Preheat the air fryer to 390°F (199°C). Grease the air fryer basket with olive oil.
2. On a clean work surface, rub the chicken drumsticks with Cajun seasoning, salt, and ground black pepper.
3. Arrange the seasoned chicken drumsticks in a single layer in the air fryer. You need to work in batches to avoid overcrowding.
4. Air fry for 18 minutes or until lightly browned. Flip the drumsticks halfway through.
5. Remove the chicken drumsticks from the air fryer. Serve immediately.

Air Fried Chicken Wings with Buffalo Sauce

Prep time: 10 minutes | Cook time: 20 minutes | Serves 6

* 16 chicken drumettes (party wings)
* Chicken seasoning or rub, to taste
* 1 teaspoon garlic powder
* Ground black pepper, to taste
* ¼ cup buffalo wings sauce
* Cooking spray

1. Preheat the air fryer to 400°F (204°C). Spritz the air fryer basket with cooking spray.
2. Rub the chicken wings with chicken seasoning, garlic powder, and ground black pepper on a clean work surface.
3. Arrange the chicken wings in the preheated air fryer. Spritz with cooking spray. Air fry for 10 minutes or until lightly browned. Shake the basket halfway through.
4. Transfer the chicken wings in a large bowl, then pour in the buffalo wings sauce and toss to coat well.
5. Put the wings back to the air fryer and cook for an additional 7 minutes.
6. Serve immediately.

Rosemary Turkey Scotch Eggs (Air Fryer)

Prep time: 15 minutes | Cook time: 12 minutes | Serves 4

- 1 egg
- 1 cup panko bread crumbs
- ½ teaspoon rosemary
- 1 pound (454 g) ground turkey
- 4 hard-boiled eggs, peeled
- Salt and ground black pepper, to taste
- Cooking spray

1. Preheat the air fryer to 400ºF (204ºC). Spritz the air fryer basket with cooking spray.
2. Whisk the egg with salt in a bowl. Combine the bread crumbs with rosemary in a shallow dish.
3. Stir the ground turkey with salt and ground black pepper in a separate large bowl, then divide the ground turkey into four portions.
4. Wrap each hard-boiled egg with a portion of ground turkey. Dredge in the whisked egg, then roll over the breadcrumb mixture.
5. Place the wrapped eggs in the preheated air fryer and spritz with cooking spray. Air fry for 12 minutes or until golden brown and crunchy. Flip the eggs halfway through.
6. Serve immediately.

Strawberry-Glazed Turkey (Air Fryer)

Prep time: 15 minutes | Cook time: 37 minutes | Serves 2

- 2 pounds (907 g) turkey breast
- 1 tablespoon olive oil
- Salt and ground black pepper, to
- taste
- 1 cup fresh strawberries

1. Preheat the air fryer to 375ºF (191ºC).
2. Rub the turkey bread with olive oil on a clean work surface, then sprinkle with salt and ground black pepper.
3. Transfer the turkey in the preheated air fryer and air fry for 30 minutes or until the internal temperature of the turkey reaches at least 165ºF (74ºC). flip the turkey breast halfway through.
4. Meanwhile, put the strawberries in a food processor and pulse until smooth.
5. When the frying of the turkey is complete, spread the puréed strawberries over the turkey and fry for 7 more minutes.
6. Serve immediately.

Air Fried Chicken Potatoes with Sun-Dried Tomato

Prep time: 15 minutes | Cook time: 25 minutes | Serves 2

- 2 teaspoons minced fresh oregano, divided
- 2 teaspoons minced fresh thyme, divided
- 2 teaspoons extra-virgin olive oil, plus extra as needed
- 1 pound (454 g) fingerling potatoes, unpeeled
- 2 (12-ounce / 340-g) bone-in split chicken breasts, trimmed
- 1 garlic clove, minced
- ¼ cup oil-packed sun-dried tomatoes, patted dry and chopped
- 1½ tablespoons red wine vinegar
- 1 tablespoon capers, rinsed and minced
- 1 small shallot, minced
- Salt and ground black pepper, to taste

1. Preheat the air fryer to 350ºF (177ºC).
2. Combine 1 teaspoon of oregano, 1 teaspoon of thyme, ¼ teaspoon of salt, ¼ teaspoon of ground black pepper, 1 teaspoons of olive oil in a large bowl. Add the potatoes and toss to coat well.
3. Combine the chicken with remaining thyme, oregano, and olive oil. Sprinkle with garlic, salt, and pepper. Toss to coat well.
4. Place the potatoes in the preheated air fryer, then arrange the chicken on top of the potatoes.
5. Air fry for 25 minutes or until the internal temperature of the chicken reaches at least 165ºF (74ºC) and the potatoes are wilted. Flip the chicken and potatoes halfway through.
6. Meanwhile, combine the sun-dried tomatoes, vinegar, capers, and shallot in a separate large bowl. Sprinkle with salt and ground black pepper. Toss to mix well.
7. Remove the chicken and potatoes from the air fryer and allow to cool for 10 minutes. Serve with the sun-dried tomato mix.

Chapter 6 Red Meat

Cocoa and Chili Pork (Pressure Cook)

Prep time: 10 minutes | Cook time: 30 minutes | Serves 4

- ❀ 4 pork chops
- ❀ 2 tablespoons hot sauce
- ❀ 2 tablespoons cocoa powder
- ❀ 2 teaspoons chili powder

- ❀ 1 cup beef stock
- ❀ ¼ teaspoon ground cumin
- ❀ 1 tablespoon chopped parsley
- ❀ A pinch of salt and black pepper

1. Stir together all the ingredients in your Instant Pot.
2. Secure the lid. Press the Pressure Cook on the Instant Pot and set the cooking time for 30 minutes at High Pressure.
3. Once cooking is complete, perform a natural pressure release for 10 minutes and then release any remaining pressure. Carefully open the lid.
4. Divide the mix among the plates and serve with a side salad.

Pork Cutlets with Creamy Mustard Sauce (Pressure Cook)

Prep time: 20 minutes | Cook time: 13 minutes | Serves 6

- ❀ 6 pork cutlets
- ❀ ½ teaspoon dried rosemary
- ❀ ½ teaspoon dried marjoram
- ❀ ¼ teaspoon paprika
- ❀ ¼ teaspoon cayenne pepper
- ❀ Kosher salt and ground black pepper, to taste

- ❀ 2 tablespoons olive oil
- ❀ ½ cup water
- ❀ ½ cup vegetable broth
- ❀ 1 tablespoon butter
- ❀ 1 cup heavy cream
- ❀ 1 tablespoon yellow mustard
- ❀ ½ cup shredded Cheddar cheese

1. Sprinkle both sides of the pork cutlets with rosemary, marjoram, paprika, cayenne pepper, salt, and black pepper.
2. Press the Sauté button on the Instant Pot and heat the olive oil until sizzling.
3. Add the pork cutlets and sear both sides for about 3 minutes until lightly browned.
4. Pour in the water and vegetable broth.
5. Secure the lid. Select the Pressure Cook and set the cooking time for 8 minutes at High Pressure.
6. When the timer beeps, perform a quick pressure release. Carefully open the lid. Transfer the pork cutlets to a plate and set aside.
7. Press the Sauté button again and melt the butter.
8. Stir in the heavy cream, mustard, and cheese and cook for another 2 minutes until heated through.
9. Add the pork cutlets to the sauce, turning to coat.
10. Remove from the Instant Pot and serve.

Pork Chops with Bell Peppers (Pressure Cook)

Prep time: 10 minutes | Cook time: 35 minutes | Serves 4

- 2 tablespoons olive oil
- 4 pork chops
- 1 red onion, chopped
- 3 garlic cloves, minced
- 1 red bell pepper, roughly chopped
- 1 green bell pepper, roughly chopped
- 2 cups beef stock
- A pinch of salt and black pepper
- 1 tablespoon parsley, chopped

1. Press the Sauté on your Instant Pot. Add and heat the oil. Brown the pork chops for 2 minutes.
2. Fold in the onion and garlic and brown for an additional 3 minutes.
3. Stir in the bell peppers, stock, salt, and pepper.
4. Lock the lid. Select the Pressure Cook and cook for 30 minutes at High Pressure.
5. Once cooking is complete, use a natural pressure release for 10 minutes and then release any remaining pressure. Carefully open the lid.
6. Divide the mix among the plates and serve topped with the parsley.

Curry Pork Steak (Pressure Cook)

Prep time: 15 minutes | Cook time: 15 minutes | Serves 6

- 1 teaspoon cumin seeds
- 1 teaspoon fennel seeds
- ½ teaspoon mustard seeds
- 2 chili peppers, deseeded and minced
- 1 teaspoon mixed peppercorns
- ½ teaspoon ground bay leaf
- 1 tablespoon sesame oil
- 1½ pounds (680 g) pork steak, sliced
- 1 cup chicken broth
- 3 tablespoons coconut cream
- 2 tablespoons balsamic vinegar
- 2 tablespoons chopped scallions
- 2 cloves garlic, finely minced
- 1 teaspoon curry powder
- 1 teaspoon grated fresh ginger
- ¼ teaspoon crushed red pepper flakes
- ¼ teaspoon ground black pepper
- 1 cup vegetable broth
- Sea salt, to taste

1. Heat a skillet over medium-high heat and roast the cumin seeds, fennel seeds, mustard seeds, peppers, peppercorns, and ground bay leaf and until aromatic.
2. Set the Instant Pot to Sauté. Add and heat the sesame oil until sizzling. Sear the pork steak until nicely browned.
3. Stir in the roasted seasonings and the remaining ingredients.
4. Lock the lid. Select the Pressure Cook and set the cooking time for 8 minutes at High Pressure.
5. When the timer beeps, do a quick pressure release. Carefully open the lid.
6. Divide the mix among bowls and serve immediately.

Cinnamon and Orange Pork (Pressure Cook)

Prep time: 10 minutes | Cook time: 35 minutes | Serves 4

* 4 pork chops
* 1 tablespoon cinnamon powder
* 3 garlic cloves, minced
* ½ cup beef stock

* Juice of 1 orange
* 1 tablespoon grated ginger
* 1 teaspoon dried rosemary
* A pinch of salt and black pepper

1. Stir together all the ingredients in your Instant Pot.
2. Secure the lid. Press the Pressure Cook on the Instant Pot and set the cooking time for 35 minutes at High Pressure.
3. Once cooking is complete, perform a natural pressure release for 10 minutes and then release any remaining pressure. Carefully open the lid.
4. Divide the mix among the plates and serve immediately.

Beef Rice Noodles (Pressure Cook)

Prep time: 15 minutes | Cook time: 16 minutes | Serves 4

* 6 cups boiled water
* 8 ounces (227 g) rice noodles
* 1 tablespoon sesame oil
* 1 pound (454 g) ground beef
* 2 cups sliced shitake mushrooms

* ½ cup julienned carrots
* 1 yellow onion, sliced
* 1 cup shredded green cabbage
* ¼ cup sliced scallions, for garnish
* Sesame seeds, for garnish

Sauce:
* ¼ cup tamarind sauce
* 1 tablespoon hoisin sauce

* 1 teaspoon grated ginger
* 1 teaspoon maple syrup

1. In a medium bowl, whisk together the ingredients for the sauce. Set aside.
2. Pour boiling water into a bowl and add rice noodles. Cover the bowl and allow the noodles to soften for 5 minutes. Drain and set aside.
3. Set the Instant Pot to Sauté mode and heat the sesame oil.
4. Cook the beef in the pot for 5 minutes or until browned.
5. Stir in the mushrooms, carrots, onion, and cabbage. Cook for 5 minutes or until softened.
6. Add the noodles. Top with the sauce and mix well. Cook for 1 more minute. Garnish with scallions and sesame seeds and serve immediately.

Pork, Green Beans, and Corn (Pressure Cook)

Prep time: 10 minutes | Cook time: 35 minutes | Serves 4

* 2 pounds (907 g) pork shoulder, boneless and cubed
* 1 cup green beans, trimmed and halved
* 1 cup corn
* 1 cup beef stock
* 2 garlic cloves, minced
* 1 teaspoon ground cumin
* A pinch of salt and black pepper

1. Combine all the ingredients in the Instant Pot.
2. Secure the lid. Select the Pressure Cook and set the cooking time for 35 minutes at High Pressure.
3. Once cooking is complete, do a natural pressure release for 10 minutes, then release any remaining pressure. Carefully open the lid.
4. Divide the mix among four plates and serve.

Pork Meatloaf (Pressure Cook)

Prep time: 10 minutes | Cook time: 30 minutes | Serves 4

* 2 pounds (907 g) ground pork meat
* ½ cup tomato sauce
* ½ cup almond meal
* ½ cup coconut milk
* 2 eggs, whisked
* 1 yellow onion, minced
* 1 tablespoon chopped parsley
* 1 tablespoon chopped chives
* A pinch of salt and black pepper
* 2 cups water

1. Stir together all the ingredients except the water in a large mixing bowl until well incorporated.
2. Form the mixture into a meatloaf and transfer to a loaf pan that fits the Instant Pot.
3. Pour the water into the Instant Pot and insert a steamer basket. Place the loaf pan in the basket.
4. Lock the lid. Select the Pressure Cook and set the cooking time for 30 minutes at High Pressure.
5. Once cooking is complete, do a natural pressure release for 10 minutes, then release any remaining pressure. Carefully open the lid.
6. Allow to cool for 5 minutes before slicing and serving.

Beef and Broccoli (Pressure Cook)

Prep time: 15 minutes | Cook time: 25 minutes | Serves 4

- ½ cup grass-fed bone broth
- 1 pound (454 g) chuck steak, sliced
- 1 jalapeño pepper, sliced
- 1 green onion, chopped
- ½ teaspoon ginger, grated
- ½ teaspoon garlic
- 2 tablespoons coconut oil
- ½ teaspoon crushed red pepper
- ½ teaspoon kosher salt
- ½ teaspoon freshly ground black pepper
- ½ teaspoon dried parsley
- 1 cup broccoli, chopped
- 1 teaspoon sesame seeds

1. Pour the bone broth into the Instant Pot, then add the steak, jalapeño, green onion, ginger, garlic, coconut oil, red pepper, salt, black pepper, and parsley.
2. Close the lid and select the Pressure Cook. Set the cooking time for 20 minutes at High Pressure.
3. When timer beeps, let the pressure naturally release for about 10 minutes, then release any remaining pressure. Carefully open the lid.
4. Transfer the steak mixture on a plate. Add the broccoli and set to the Sauté mode. Cook for 5 minutes or until tender. Remove the broccoli from the pot.
5. Top the beef with the sesame seeds, serve with the broccoli.

Beef Meatballs with Roasted Tomatoes (Pressure Cook)

Prep time: 15 minutes | Cook time: 16 minutes | Serves 4

- 2 tablespoons avocado oil
- 1 pound (454 g) ground beef
- ½ teaspoon dried basil
- ½ teaspoon crushed red pepper
- ½ teaspoon ground cayenne pepper
- ½ teaspoon kosher salt
- ½ teaspoon freshly ground black pepper
- 2 (14-ounce / 397-g) cans fire roasted tomatoes

1. Set the Instant Pot to Sauté mode and heat the avocado oil.
2. In a large bowl, mix the remaining ingredients, except for the tomatoes. Form the mixture into 1½-inch meatballs and place them into the Instant Pot. Spread the tomatoes evenly over the meatballs.
3. Close the lid. Select the Pressure Cook, set the cooking time for 16 minutes at High Pressure.
4. When timer beeps, perform a natural pressure release for 5 minutes, then release any remaining pressure.
5. Open the lid and serve.

Beef Roast with Cauliflower (Pressure Cook)

Prep time: 10 minutes | Cook time: 15 minutes | Serves 2

- 2 teaspoons sesame oil
- 12 ounces (340 g) sliced beef roast
- Freshly ground black pepper, to taste
- ½ small onion, chopped
- 3 garlic cloves, minced
- ½ cup beef stock
- ¼ cup soy sauce
- 2 tablespoons brown sugar
- Pinch red pepper flakes
- 1 tablespoon cornstarch
- 8 ounces (227 g) fresh cauliflower, cut into florets

1. Set the Instant Pot pot on Sauté mode. Add the sesame oil, beef, and black pepper. Sear for 2 minutes on all sides. Transfer the beef to a plate and set aside.
2. Add the onion and garlic to the pot and sauté for 2 minutes or until softened.
3. Stir in the stock, soy sauce, brown sugar, and red pepper flakes. Stir until the sugar is dissolved, then return the beef to the pot.
4. Secure the lid and set to the Pressure Cook. Set the cooking time for 10 minutes at High Pressure.
5. When timer beeps, quick release the pressure and open the lid. Set to the Sauté mode.
6. Transfer 2 tablespoons of liquid from the pot to a small bowl. Whisk it with the cornstarch, then add back to the pot along with the cauliflower.
7. Cover the lid and let simmer for 3 to 4 minutes, or until the sauce is thickened and the cauliflower is softened.
8. Serve the beef and cauliflower.

Spicy Minced Lamb Meat (Pressure Cook)

Prep time: 10 minutes | Cook time: 20 minutes | Serves 2

- ½ pound (227 g) ground lamb meat
- ½ cup onion, chopped
- ½ tablespoon minced ginger
- ½ tablespoon garlic
- ½ teaspoon salt
- ¼ teaspoon ground coriander
- ¼ teaspoon cayenne pepper
- ¼ teaspoon cumin
- ¼ teaspoon turmeric

1. Press the Sauté button on the Instant Pot. Add the onion, ginger and garlic to the pot and sauté for 5 minutes. Add the remaining ingredients to the pot and lock the lid.
2. Select the Pressure Cook and set the cooking time for 15 minutes at High Pressure. Once the timer goes off, perform a natural pressure release for 15 minutes.
3. Open the lid and serve immediately.

Beef Steaks with Mushrooms (Pressure Cook)

Prep time: 15 minutes | Cook time: 25 minutes | Serves 2

- ❁ 2 beef steaks, boneless
- ❁ Salt and black pepper, to taste
- ❁ 2 tablespoons olive oil
- ❁ 4 ounces (113 g) mushrooms, sliced
- ❁ ½ onion, chopped
- ❁ 1 garlic clove, minced
- ❁ 1 cup vegetable soup
- ❁ 1½ tablespoons cornstarch
- ❁ 1 tablespoon half-and-half

1. Rub the beef steaks with salt and pepper on a clean work surface.
2. Set the Instant Pot to Sauté mode and warm the olive oil until shimmering.
3. Sear the beef for 2 minutes per side until browned. Transfer to a plate.
4. Add the mushrooms and sauté for 5 minutes or until soft. Add the onion and garlic and sauté for 2 minutes until fragrant.
5. Return the steaks to the pot and pour in the soup. Seal the lid, select the Pressure Cook, and set the time to 15 minutes at High Pressure.
6. When cooking is complete, do a quick pressure release and unlock the lid and transfer the chops to a plate. Press the Sauté button.
7. In a bowl, combine the cornstarch and half-and-half and mix well. Pour the mixture into the pot and cook until the sauce is thickened. Serve warm.

Mexican Beef Shred (Pressure Cook)

Prep time: 20 minutes | Cook time: 30 minutes | Serves 4

- ❁ 1 pound (454 g) tender chuck roast, cut into half
- ❁ 3 tablespoons chipotle sauce
- ❁ 1 (8-ounce / 227-g) can tomato sauce
- ❁ 1 cup beef broth
- ❁ ½ cup chopped cilantro
- ❁ 1 lime, zested and juiced
- ❁ 2 teaspoons cumin powder
- ❁ 1 teaspoon cayenne pepper
- ❁ Salt and ground black pepper, to taste
- ❁ ½ teaspoon garlic powder
- ❁ 1 tablespoon olive oil

1. In the Instant Pot, add the beef, chipotle sauce, tomato sauce, beef broth, cilantro, lime zest, lime juice, cumin powder, cayenne pepper, salt, pepper, and garlic powder.
2. Seal the lid, then select the Pressure Cook and set the cooking time for 30 minutes at High Pressure.
3. Once cooking is complete, allow a natural pressure release for 10 minutes, then release any remaining pressure.
4. Unlock the lid and using two forks to shred the beef into strands. Stir in the olive oil. Serve warm.

Italian Steak and Spinach Rolls (Air Fryer)

Prep time: 50 minutes | Cook time: 9 minutes | Serves 4

- 2 teaspoons dried Italian seasoning
- 2 cloves garlic, minced
- 1 tablespoon vegetable oil
- 1 teaspoon kosher salt
- 1 teaspoon ground black pepper
- 1 pound (454 g) flank steak, ¼ to ½ inch thick
- 1 (10-ounce / 284-g) package frozen spinach, thawed and squeezed dry
- ½ cup diced jarred roasted red pepper
- 1 cup shredded Mozzarella cheese
- Cooking spray

1. Combine the Italian seasoning, garlic, vegetable oil, salt, and ground black pepper in a large bowl. Stir to mix well.
2. Dunk the steak in the seasoning mixture and toss to coat well. Wrap the bowl in plastic and marinate under room temperature for at least 30 minutes.
3. Preheat the air fryer to 400ºF (204ºC). Spritz the air fryer basket with cooking spray.
4. Remove the marinated steak from the bowl and unfold on a clean work surface, then spread the top of the steak with a layer of spinach, a layer of red pepper and a layer of cheese. Leave a ¼-inch edge uncovered.
5. Roll the steak up to wrap the filling, then secure with 3 toothpicks. Cut the roll in half and transfer the rolls in the preheated air fryer basket, seam side down.
6. Air fry for 9 minutes or until the steak is lightly browned and the internal temperature reaches at least 145ºF (63ºC).
7. Remove the rolls from the air fryer and slice to serve.

Thai Curry Beef Meatballs (Air Fryer)

Prep time: 5 minutes | Cook time: 15 minutes | Serves 4

- 1 pound (454 g) ground beef
- 1 tablespoon sesame oil
- 2 teaspoons chopped lemongrass
- 1 teaspoon red Thai curry paste
- 1 teaspoon Thai seasoning blend
- Juice and zest of ½ lime
- Cooking spray

1. Preheat the air fryer to 380ºF (193ºC). Spritz the air fryer basket with cooking spray.
2. In a medium bowl, combine all the ingredients until well blended.
3. Shape the meat mixture into 24 meatballs and arrange them in the air fryer basket. Air fry for 15 minutes, or until well browned. Flip halfway through to ensure even cooking.
4. Transfer the meatballs to plates. Let cool for 5 minutes before serving.

Mongolian Arrowroot Glazed Beef (Pressure Cook)

Prep time: 15 minutes | Cook time: 20 minutes | Serves 4

❀ 1 tablespoon sesame oil
❀ 1 (2-pound / 907-g) skirt steak, sliced into thin strips
❀ ½ cup pure maple syrup
❀ ¼ cup soy sauce
❀ 4 cloves garlic, minced

❀ 1-inch knob fresh ginger root, peeled and grated
❀ ½ cup plus 2 tablespoons water, divided
❀ 2 tablespoons arrowroot powder

1. Press the Sauté button on the Instant Pot. Heat the sesame oil.
2. Add and sear the steak strips for 3 minutes on all sides.
3. In a medium bowl, whisk together maple syrup, soy sauce, garlic, ginger, and ½ cup water. Pour the mixture over beef. Lock the lid.
4. Press the Pressure Cook and set the cooking time for 10 minutes at High Pressure.
5. When timer beeps, quick release the pressure, then unlock the lid.
6. Meanwhile, in a small dish, whisk together the arrowroot and 2 tablespoons water until smooth and chunky.
7. Stir the arrowroot into the beef mixture. Press the Sauté button and simmer for 5 minutes or until the sauce thickens.
8. Ladle the beef and sauce on plates and serve.

New York Strip with Heavy Cream (Pressure Cook)

Prep time: 15 minutes | Cook time: 30 minutes | Serves 4

❀ 1 tablespoon sesame oil
❀ 1 pound (454 g) New York strip, sliced into thin strips
❀ ½ leek, sliced
❀ 1 carrot, sliced
❀ ⅓ cup dry red wine

❀ ½ tablespoon tamari
❀ ½ cup cream of mushroom soup
❀ 1 clove garlic, sliced
❀ Kosher salt and ground black pepper, to taste
❀ ¼ cup heavy cream

1. Press the Sauté button of the Instant Pot. Heat the sesame oil until sizzling.
2. Add and brown the beef strips in batches for 4 minutes. Stir in the remaining ingredients, except for the heavy cream.
3. Secure the lid. Choose the Pressure Cook and set the cooking time for 20 minutes at High pressure.
4. Once cooking is complete, use a quick pressure release. Carefully open the lid.
5. Transfer the beef on a serving plate. Mash the vegetables in the pot with a potato masher.
6. Press the Sauté button. Bring to a boil, then Stir in the heavy cream.
7. Spoon the mixture over the New York strip and serve immediately.

Lamb Curry with Zucchini (Pressure Cook)

Prep time: 40 minutes | Cook time: 25 minutes | Serves 3

- 1 pound (454 g) cubed lamb stew meat
- 2 garlic cloves, minced
- ½ cup coconut milk
- 1 tablespoon grated fresh ginger
- ½ teaspoon lime juice
- ¼ teaspoon salt
- ¼ teaspoon black pepper
- 1 tablespoon olive oil
- 1½ medium carrots, sliced
- ½ medium onion, diced
- ¾ cup diced tomatoes
- ½ teaspoon turmeric powder
- ½ medium zucchini, diced

1. In a bowl, stir together the garlic, coconut milk, ginger, lime juice, salt and pepper. Add the lamb to the bowl and marinate for 30 minutes.
2. Combine the remaining ingredients, except for the zucchini, in the Instant Pot. Add the meat and the marinade to the pot.
3. Set the lid in place. Select the Pressure Cook and set the cooking time for 20 minutes at High Pressure. Once the timer goes off, use a natural pressure release for 15 minutes, then release any remaining pressure.
4. Open the lid. Add the zucchini to the pot. Select the Sauté mode and cook for 5 minutes.
5. Serve hot.

Sumptuous Lamb Casserole (Pressure Cook)

Prep time: 15 minutes | Cook time: 41 minutes | Serves 2 to 4

- 1 pound (454 g) lamb stew meat, cubed
- 1 tablespoon olive oil
- 3 cloves garlic, minced
- 2 tomatoes, chopped
- 2 carrots, chopped
- 1 onion, chopped
- 1 pound (454 g) baby potatoes
- 1 celery stalk, chopped
- 2 cups chicken stock
- 2 tablespoons red wine
- 2 tablespoons ketchup
- 1 teaspoon ground cumin
- 1 teaspoon sweet paprika
- ¼ teaspoon dried rosemary
- ¼ teaspoon dried oregano
- Salt and ground black pepper, to taste

1. Press the Sauté button on the Instant Pot and heat the oil. Add the lamb to the pot and sear for 5 minutes, or until lightly browned. Add the garlic and sauté for 1 minute. Add all the remaining ingredients to the pot.
2. Set the lid in place. Select the Pressure Cook and set the cooking time for 35 minutes at High Pressure. Once cooking is complete, perform a natural pressure release for 10 minutes, then release any remaining pressure. Carefully open the lid.
3. Serve hot.

Cinnamon-Beef Kofta (Air Fryer)

Prep time: 10 minutes | Cook time: 13 minutes | Makes 12 koftas

- ❁ 1½ pounds (680 g) lean ground beef
- ❁ 1 teaspoon onion powder
- ❁ ¾ teaspoon ground cinnamon
- ❁ ¾ teaspoon ground dried turmeric
- ❁ 1 teaspoon ground cumin
- ❁ ¾ teaspoon salt
- ❁ ¼ teaspoon cayenne
- ❁ 12 (3½- to 4-inch-long) cinnamon sticks
- ❁ Cooking spray

1. Preheat the air fryer to 375ºF (191ºC). Spritz the air fryer basket with cooking spray.
2. Combine all the ingredients, except for the cinnamon sticks, in a large bowl. Toss to mix well.
3. Divide and shape the mixture into 12 balls, then wrap each ball around each cinnamon stick and leave a quarter of the length uncovered.
4. Arrange the beef-cinnamon sticks in the preheated air fryer and spritz with cooking spray. Work in batches to avoid overcrowding.
5. Air fry for 13 minutes or until the beef is browned. Flip the sticks halfway through.
6. Serve immediately.

Teriyaki Rump Steak with Broccoli (Air Fryer)

Prep time: 5 minutes | Cook time: 13 minutes | Serves 4

- ❁ ½ pound (227 g) rump steak
- ❁ 1/3 cup teriyaki marinade
- ❁ 1½ teaspoons sesame oil
- ❁ ½ head broccoli, cut into florets
- ❁ 2 red capsicums, sliced
- ❁ Fine sea salt and ground black pepper, to taste
- ❁ Cooking spray

1. Toss the rump steak in a large bowl with teriyaki marinade. Wrap the bowl in plastic and refrigerate to marinate for at least an hour.
2. Preheat the air fryer to 400ºF (204ºC) and spritz with cooking spray.
3. Discard the marinade and transfer the steak in the preheated air fryer. Spritz with cooking spray.
4. Air fry for 13 minutes or until well browned. Flip the steak halfway through.
5. Meanwhile, heat the sesame oil in a nonstick skillet over medium heat. Add the broccoli and capsicum. Sprinkle with salt and ground black pepper. Sauté for 5 minutes or until the broccoli is tender.
6. Transfer the air fried rump steak on a plate and top with the sautéed broccoli and capsicum. Serve hot.

Spicy Pork with Candy Onions (Air Fryer)

Prep time: 10 minutes | Cook time: 52 minutes | Serves 4

- ❋ 2 teaspoons sesame oil
- ❋ 1 teaspoon dried sage, crushed
- ❋ 1 teaspoon cayenne pepper
- ❋ 1 rosemary sprig, chopped
- ❋ 1 thyme sprig, chopped
- ❋ Sea salt and ground black pepper, to taste
- ❋ 2 pounds (907 g) pork leg roast, scored
- ❋ ½ pound (227 g) candy onions, sliced
- ❋ 4 cloves garlic, finely chopped
- ❋ 2 chili peppers, minced

1. Preheat the air fryer to 400ºF (204ºC).
2. In a mixing bowl, combine the sesame oil, sage, cayenne pepper, rosemary, thyme, salt and black pepper until well mixed. In another bowl, place the pork leg and brush with the seasoning mixture.
3. Place the seasoned pork leg in a baking pan and air fry for 40 minutes, or until lightly browned, flipping halfway through. Add the candy onions, garlic and chili peppers to the pan and air fry for another 12 minutes.
4. Transfer the pork leg to a plate. Let cool for 5 minutes and slice. Spread the juices left in the pan over the pork and serve warm with the candy onions.

Spicy Pork Chops with Carrots and Mushrooms (Air Fryer)

Prep time: 10 minutes | Cook time: 15 to 18 minutes | Serves 4

- ❋ 2 carrots, cut into sticks
- ❋ 1 cup mushrooms, sliced
- ❋ 2 garlic cloves, minced
- ❋ 2 tablespoons olive oil
- ❋ 1 pound (454 g) boneless pork chops
- ❋ 1 teaspoon dried oregano
- ❋ 1 teaspoon dried thyme
- ❋ 1 teaspoon cayenne pepper
- ❋ Salt and ground black pepper, to taste
- ❋ Cooking spray

1. Preheat the air fryer to 360ºF (182ºC). Spritz the air fryer basket with cooking spray.
2. In a mixing bowl, toss together the carrots, mushrooms, garlic, olive oil and salt until well combined.
3. Add the pork chops to a different bowl and season with oregano, thyme, cayenne pepper, salt and black pepper.
4. Lower the vegetable mixture in the prepared air fryer basket. Place the seasoned pork chops on top. Air fry for 15 to 18 minutes, or until the pork is well browned and the vegetables are tender, flipping the pork and shaking the basket once halfway through.
5. Transfer the pork chops to the serving dishes and let cool for 5 minutes. Serve warm with vegetable on the side.

Stuffed Beef Tenderloin with Feta Cheese (Air Fryer)

Prep time: 10 minutes | Cook time: 10 minutes | Serves 4

- 1½ pounds (680 g) beef tenderloin, pounded to ¼ inch thick
- 3 teaspoons sea salt
- 1 teaspoon ground black pepper
- 2 ounces (57 g) creamy goat
- cheese
- ½ cup crumbled feta cheese
- ¼ cup finely chopped onions
- 2 cloves garlic, minced
- Cooking spray

1. Preheat the air fryer to 400ºF (204ºC). Spritz the air fryer basket with cooking spray.
2. Unfold the beef tenderloin on a clean work surface. Rub the salt and pepper all over the beef tenderloin to season.
3. Make the filling for the stuffed beef tenderloins: Combine the goat cheese, feta, onions, and garlic in a medium bowl. Stir until well blended.
4. Spoon the mixture in the center of the tenderloin. Roll the tenderloin up tightly like rolling a burrito and use some kitchen twine to tie the tenderloin.
5. Arrange the tenderloin in the air fryer basket and air fry for 10 minutes, flipping the tenderloin halfway through to ensure even cooking, or until an instant-read thermometer inserted in the center of the tenderloin registers 135ºF (57ºC) for medium-rare.
6. Transfer to a platter and serve immediately.

Tuscan Air Fried Veal Loin (Air Fryer)

Prep time: 1 hour 10 minutes | Cook time: 12 minutes | Makes 3 veal chops

- 1½ teaspoons crushed fennel seeds
- 1 tablespoon minced fresh rosemary leaves
- 1 tablespoon minced garlic
- 1½ teaspoons lemon zest
- 1½ teaspoons salt
- ½ teaspoon red pepper flakes
- 2 tablespoons olive oil
- 3 (10-ounce / 284-g) bone-in veal loin, about ½ inch thick

1. Combine all the ingredients, except for the veal loin, in a large bowl. Stir to mix well.
2. Dunk the loin in the mixture and press to submerge. Wrap the bowl in plastic and refrigerate for at least an hour to marinate.
3. Preheat the air fryer to 400ºF (204ºC).
4. Arrange the veal loin in the preheated air fryer and air fry for 12 minutes for medium-rare, or until it reaches your desired doneness.
5. Serve immediately.

Simple Pork Meatballs with Red Chili (Air Fryer)

Prep time: 5 minutes | Cook time: 15 minutes | Serves 4

- 1 pound (454 g) ground pork
- 2 cloves garlic, finely minced
- 1 cup scallions, finely chopped
- 1½ tablespoons Worcestershire sauce
- ½ teaspoon freshly grated ginger
- root
- 1 teaspoon turmeric powder
- 1 tablespoon oyster sauce
- 1 small sliced red chili, for garnish
- Cooking spray

1. Preheat the air fryer to 350ºF (177ºC). Spritz the air fryer basket with cooking spray.
2. Combine all the ingredients, except for the red chili in a large bowl. Toss to mix well.
3. Shape the mixture into equally sized balls, then arrange them in the preheated air fryer and spritz with cooking spray.
4. Air fry for 15 minutes or until the balls are lightly browned. Flip the balls halfway through.
5. Serve the pork meatballs with red chili on top.

Smoky Paprika Pork and Vegetable Kabobs (Air Fryer)

Prep time: 25 minutes | Cook time: 15 minutes | Serves 4

- 1 pound (454 g) pork tenderloin, cubed
- 1 teaspoon smoked paprika
- Salt and ground black pepper, to taste
- 1 green bell pepper, cut into chunks
- 1 zucchini, cut into chunks
- 1 red onion, sliced
- 1 tablespoon oregano
- Cooking spray

Special Equipment:
- Small bamboo skewers, soaked in water for 20 minutes to keep them from burning while cooking

1. Preheat the air fryer to 350ºF (177ºC). Spritz the air fryer basket with cooking spray.
2. Add the pork to a bowl and season with the smoked paprika, salt and black pepper. Thread the seasoned pork cubes and vegetables alternately onto the soaked skewers.
3. Arrange the skewers in the prepared air fryer basket and spray with cooking spray. Air fry for 15 minutes, or until the pork is well browned and the vegetables are tender, flipping once halfway through.
4. Transfer the skewers to the serving dishes and sprinkle with oregano. Serve hot.

Lamb Kofta (Air Fryer)

Prep time: 25 minutes | Cook time: 10 minutes | Serves 4

* 1 pound (454 g) ground lamb
* 1 tablespoon ras el hanout (North African spice)
* ½ teaspoon ground coriander
* 1 teaspoon onion powder
* 1 teaspoon garlic powder
* 1 teaspoon cumin
* 2 tablespoons mint, chopped
* Salt and ground black pepper, to taste

Special Equipment:
* 4 bamboo skewers

1. Combine the ground lamb, ras el hanout, coriander, onion powder, garlic powder, cumin, mint, salt, and ground black pepper in a large bowl. Stir to mix well.
2. Transfer the mixture into sausage molds and sit the bamboo skewers in the mixture. Refrigerate for 15 minutes.
3. Preheat the air fryer to 380ºF (193ºC). Spritz the basket with cooking spray.
4. Place the lamb skewers in the preheated air fryer and spritz with cooking spray.
5. Air fry for 10 minutes or until the lamb is well browned. Flip the lamb skewers halfway through.
6. Serve immediately.

Lamb Rack with Pistachio (Air Fryer)

Prep time: 10 minutes | Cook time: 20 minutes | Serves 2

* ½ cup finely chopped pistachios
* 1 teaspoon chopped fresh rosemary
* 3 tablespoons panko bread crumbs
* 2 teaspoons chopped fresh oregano
* 1 tablespoon olive oil
* Salt and freshly ground black pepper, to taste
* 1 lamb rack, bones fat trimmed and frenched
* 1 tablespoon Dijon mustard

1. Preheat the air fryer to 380ºF (193ºC).
2. Put the pistachios, rosemary, bread crumbs, oregano, olive oil, salt, and black pepper in a food processor. Pulse to combine until smooth.
3. Rub the lamb rack with salt and black pepper on a clean work surface, then place it in the preheated air fryer.
4. Air fry for 12 minutes or until lightly browned. Flip the lamb halfway through the cooking time.
5. Transfer the lamb on a plate and brush with Dijon mustard on the fat side, then sprinkle with the pistachios mixture over the lamb rack to coat well.
6. Put the lamb rack back to the air fryer and air fry for 8 more minutes or until the internal temperature of the rack reaches at least 145ºF (63ºC).
7. Remove the lamb rack from the air fryer with tongs and allow to cool for 5 minutes before sling to serve.

Lamb Loin Chops with Horseradish Cream Sauce (Air Fryer)

Prep time: 10 minutes | Cook time: 13 minutes | Serves 4

For the Lamb:
* 4 lamb loin chops
* 2 tablespoons vegetable oil
* 1 clove garlic, minced
* ½ teaspoon kosher salt
* ½ teaspoon black pepper

For the Horseradish Cream Sauce:
* 1 to 1½ tablespoons prepared horseradish
* 1 tablespoon Dijon mustard
* ½ cup mayonnaise
* 2 teaspoons sugar
* Cooking spray

1. Preheat the air fryer to 325ºF (163ºC). Spritz the air fryer basket with cooking spray.
2. Place the lamb chops on a plate. Rub with the oil and sprinkle with the garlic, salt and black pepper. Let sit to marinate for 30 minutes at room temperature.
3. Make the horseradish cream sauce: Mix the horseradish, mustard, mayonnaise, and sugar in a bowl until well combined. Set half of the sauce aside until ready to serve.
4. Arrange the marinated chops in the prepared basket. Set the time to 10 minutes, flipping the chops halfway through.
5. Transfer the chops from the air fryer to the bowl of the horseradish sauce. Roll to coat well.
6. Put the coated chops in the air fryer basket again. Set the temperature to 400ºF (204ºC) and the time to 3 minutes. Air fry until the internal temperature reaches 145ºF (63ºC) on a meat thermometer (for medium-rare).
7. Serve hot with the horseradish cream sauce.

Lush Salisbury Steak with Mushroom Gravy (Air Fryer)

Prep time: 20 minutes | Cook time: 33 minutes | Serves 2

For the Mushroom Gravy:
* ¾ cup sliced button mushrooms
* ¼ cup thinly sliced onions
* ¼ cup unsalted butter, melted
* ½ teaspoon fine sea salt
* ¼ cup beef broth

For the Steaks:
* ½ pound (227 g) ground beef (85% lean)
* 1 tablespoon dry mustard
* 2 tablespoons tomato paste
* ¼ teaspoon garlic powder
* ½ teaspoon onion powder
* ½ teaspoon fine sea salt
* ¼ teaspoon ground black pepper
* Chopped fresh thyme leaves, for garnish

1. Preheat the air fryer to 390°F (199°C).
2. Toss the mushrooms and onions with butter in a baking pan to coat well, then sprinkle with salt.
3. Place the baking pan in the preheated air fryer and bake for 8 minutes or until the mushrooms are tender. Stir the mixture halfway through.
4. Pour the broth in the baking pan and bake for 10 more minutes to make the gravy.
5. Meanwhile, combine all the ingredients for the steaks, except for the thyme leaves, in a large bowl. Stir to mix well. Shape the mixture into two oval steaks.
6. Arrange the steaks over the gravy and bake for 15 minutes or until the patties are browned. Flip the steaks halfway through.
7. Transfer the steaks onto a plate and pour the gravy over. Sprinkle with fresh thyme and serve immediately.

Chapter 7 Fish and Seafood

Lime Tilapia Fillets (Pressure Cook)

Prep time: 10 minutes | Cook time: 2 minutes | Serves 4

* 1 cup water
* 4 tablespoons lime juice
* 3 tablespoons chili powder

* ½ teaspoon salt
* 1 pound (454 g) tilapia fillets

1. Pour the water into Instant Pot and insert a trivet.
2. Whisk together the lime juice, chili powder, and salt in a small bowl until combined. Brush both sides of the tilapia fillets generously with the sauce. Put the tilapia fillets on top of the trivet.
3. Secure the lid. Select the Pressure Cook and set the cooking time for 2 minutes at High Pressure.
4. Once cooking is complete, do a quick pressure release. Carefully open the lid.
5. Remove the tilapia fillets from the Instant Pot to a plate and serve.

Steamed Cod and Veggies (Pressure Cook)

Prep time: 5 minutes | Cook time: 2 to 4 minutes | Serves 2

* ½ cup water
* Kosher salt and freshly ground black pepper, to taste
* 2 tablespoons freshly squeezed lemon juice, divided
* 2 tablespoons melted butter
* 1 garlic clove, minced
* 1 zucchini or yellow summer
squash, cut into thick slices
* 1 cup cherry tomatoes
* 1 cup whole Brussels sprouts
* 2 (6-ounce / 170-g) cod fillets
* 2 thyme sprigs or ½ teaspoon dried thyme
* Hot cooked rice, for serving

1. Pour the water into your Instant Pot and insert a steamer basket.
2. Sprinkle the fish with the salt and pepper. Mix together 1 tablespoon of the lemon juice, the butter, and garlic in a small bowl. Set aside.
3. Add the zucchini, tomatoes, and Brussels sprouts to the basket. Sprinkle with the salt and pepper and drizzle the remaining 1 tablespoon of lemon juice over the top.
4. Place the fish fillets on top of the veggies. Brush with the mixture and then turn the fish and repeat on the other side. Drizzle any remaining mixture all over the veggies. Place the thyme sprigs on top.
5. Lock the lid. Select the Steam mode and set the cooking time for 2 to 4 minutes at High Pressure, depending on the thickness of the fish.
6. Once cooking is complete, use a quick pressure release. Carefully open the lid.
7. Serve the cod and veggies over the cooked rice.

Easy Steamed Salmon (Pressure Cook)

Prep time: 5 minutes | Cook time: 10 minutes | Serves 2

* 1 cup water
* 2 salmon fillets
* Salt and ground black pepper, to taste

1. Pour the water into the Instant Pot and add a trivet.
2. Season the salmon fillets with salt and black pepper to taste. Put the salmon fillets on the trivet.
3. Secure the lid. Select the Steam mode and set the cooking time for 10 minutes at High Pressure.
4. Once cooking is complete, do a natural pressure release for 10 minutes, then release any remaining pressure. Carefully open the lid.
5. Serve hot.

Shrimp Spaghetti with Parmesan (Pressure Cook)

Prep time: 5 minutes | Cook time: 10 minutes | Serves 4

* 6 tablespoons butter, divided
* 12 ounces (340 g) small shrimp, peeled and deveined
* ½ teaspoon salt
* 4 cups chicken broth
* 1 pound (454 g) spaghetti
* 1 cup grated Parmesan cheese
* 1 cup heavy whipping cream
* 1 teaspoon lemon pepper

1. Set your Instant Pot to Sauté and add 2 tablespoons of butter.
2. Add the shrimp and salt to the Instant Pot and sauté for 4 minutes, or until the flesh is pink and opaque. Remove the shrimp and set aside.
3. Add the broth and scrape up any bits on the bottom of the pot.
4. Break the spaghetti in half and add to the pot. Place the remaining 4 tablespoons of butter on top.
5. Secure the lid. Press the Pressure Cook on the Instant Pot and cook for 5 minutes at High Pressure.
6. Once the timer goes off, use a quick pressure release. Carefully open the lid.
7. Fold in the cooked shrimp, Parmesan, cream, and lemon pepper. Stir until thoroughly combined.
8. Transfer to a serving plate and serve hot.

Fast Salmon with Broccoli (Pressure Cook)

Prep time: 5 minutes | Cook time: 5 minutes | Serves 2

- 1 cup water
- 8 ounces (227 g) salmon fillets
- 8 ounces (227 g) broccoli, cut into florets
- Salt and ground black pepper, to taste

1. Pour the water into the Instant Pot and insert a trivet.
2. Season the salmon and broccoli florets with salt and pepper. Put them on the trivet.
3. Secure the lid. Select the Steam mode and set the cooking time for 5 minutes at High Pressure.
4. Once cooking is complete, do a natural pressure release for 10 minutes, then release any remaining pressure. Carefully open the lid.
5. Serve hot.

Easy Shrimp and Vegetable Paella (Air Fryer)

Prep time: 5 minutes | Cook time: 14 to 17 minutes | Serves 4

- 1 (10-ounce / 284-g) package frozen cooked rice, thawed
- 1 (6-ounce / 170-g) jar artichoke hearts, drained and chopped
- ¼ cup vegetable broth
- ½ teaspoon dried thyme
- ½ teaspoon turmeric
- 1 cup frozen cooked small shrimp
- ½ cup frozen baby peas
- 1 tomato, diced

1. Preheat the air fryer to 340ºF (171ºC).
2. Mix together the cooked rice, chopped artichoke hearts, vegetable broth, thyme, and turmeric in a baking pan and stir to combine.
3. Put the baking pan in the preheated air fryer and bake for about 9 minutes, or until the rice is heated through.
4. Remove the pan from the air fryer and fold in the shrimp, baby peas, and diced tomato and mix well.
5. Return to the air fryer and continue cooking for 5 to 8 minutes, or until the shrimp are done and the paella is bubbling.
6. Cool for 5 minutes before serving.

Creamy Tuna and Eggs (Pressure Cook)

Prep time: 5 minutes | Cook time: 15 minutes | Serves 4

- 2 cans tuna, drained
- 2 eggs, beaten
- 1 can cream of celery soup
- 2 carrots, peeled and chopped
- 1 cup frozen peas
- ½ cup water
- ¾ cup milk
- ¼ cup diced onions
- 2 tablespoons butter
- Salt and ground black pepper, to taste

1. Combine all the ingredients in the Instant Pot and stir to mix well.
2. Secure the lid. Select the Pressure Cook and set the cooking time for 15 minutes at High Pressure.
3. Once cooking is complete, do a quick pressure release. Carefully open the lid.
4. Divide the mix into bowls and serve.

Cod with Orange Sauce (Pressure Cook)

Prep time: 10 minutes | Cook time: 7 minutes | Serves 4

- 4 cod fillets, boneless
- 1 cup white wine
- Juice from 1 orange
- A small grated ginger piece
- Salt and ground black pepper, to taste
- 4 spring onions, chopped

1. Combine the wine, orange juice, and ginger in your Instant Pot and stir well.
2. Insert a steamer basket. Arrange the cod fillets on the basket. Sprinkle with the salt and pepper.
3. Secure the lid. Press the Pressure Cook on your Instant Pot and set the cooking time for 7 minutes at High Pressure.
4. Once the timer beeps, do a quick pressure release. Carefully remove the lid.
5. Drizzle the sauce all over the fish and sprinkle with the green onions.
6. Transfer to a serving plate and serve immediately.

Curry-Flavored Shrimp (Pressure Cook)

Prep time: 10 minutes | Cook time: 4 minutes | Serves 2 to 4

* 2 cups water
* 1 pound (454 g) shrimp, peeled and deveined
* 8 ounces (227 g) unsweetened coconut milk
* 1 teaspoon curry powder
* 1 tablespoon garlic, minced
* Salt and ground black pepper, to taste

1. Pour the water into the Instant Pot and insert a trivet.
2. Mix together the shrimp, coconut milk, curry powder, and garlic in a large bowl. Sprinkle with the salt and pepper.
3. Add the mixture to the pan and place the dish onto the trivet, uncovered.
4. Secure the lid. Press the Pressure Cook on the Instant Pot and cook for 4 minutes at Low Pressure.
5. Once cooking is complete, use a quick pressure release. Carefully open the lid.
6. Stir well and serve.

Lemony Shrimp (Pressure Cook)

Prep time: 10 minutes | Cook time: 3 minutes | Serves 4 to 6

* 2 tablespoons butter
* 1 tablespoon lemon juice
* 1 tablespoon garlic, minced
* ½ cup chicken stock
* ½ cup white wine
* 2 pounds (907 g) shrimp
* Salt and ground black pepper, to taste
* 1 tablespoon parsley, for garnish

1. Place the butter, lemon juice, and garlic in your Instant Pot.
2. Stir in the stock and wine.
3. Add the shrimp and sprinkle with the salt and pepper. Stir well.
4. Secure the lid. Press the Pressure Cook on your Instant Pot and set the cooking time for 3 minutes at High Pressure.
5. Once the timer beeps, do a quick pressure release. Carefully remove the lid.
6. Serve topped with the parsley.

Easy Salmon Patties (Air Fryer)

Prep time: 5 minutes | Cook time: 10 t0 11 minutes | Makes 6 patties

❀ 1 (14.75-ounce / 418-g) can Alaskan pink salmon, drained and bones removed
❀ ½ cup bread crumbs
❀ 1 egg, whisked

❀ 2 scallions, diced
❀ 1 teaspoon garlic powder
❀ Salt and pepper, to taste
❀ Cooking spray

1. Preheat the air fryer to 400ºF (204ºC).
2. Stir together the salmon, bread crumbs, whisked egg, scallions, garlic powder, salt, and pepper in a large bowl until well incorporated.
3. Divide the salmon mixture into six equal portions and form each into a patty with your hands.
4. Arrange the salmon patties in the air fryer basket and spritz them with cooking spray. Air fry for 10 to 11 minutes, flipping the patties once during cooking, or until the patties are golden brown and cooked through.
5. Remove the patties from the basket and serve on a plate.

Browned Shrimp Patties (Air Fryer)

Prep time: 15 minutes | Cook time: 10 to 12 minutes | Serves 4

❀ ½ pound (227 g) raw shrimp, shelled, deveined, and chopped finely
❀ 2 cups cooked sushi rice
❀ ¼ cup chopped red bell pepper
❀ ¼ cup chopped celery
❀ ¼ cup chopped green onion

❀ 2 teaspoons Worcestershire sauce
❀ ½ teaspoon salt
❀ ½ teaspoon garlic powder
❀ ½ teaspoon Old Bay seasoning
❀ ½ cup plain bread crumbs
❀ Cooking spray

1. Preheat the air fryer to 390ºF (199ºC).
2. Put all the ingredients except the bread crumbs and oil in a large bowl and stir to incorporate.
3. Scoop out the shrimp mixture and shape into 8 equal-sized patties with your hands, no more than ½-inch thick. Roll the patties in the bread crumbs on a plate and spray both sides with cooking spray.
4. Place the patties in the air fryer basket. You may need to work in batches to avoid overcrowding.
5. Air fry for 10 to 12 minutes, flipping the patties halfway through, or until the outside is crispy brown.
6. Divide the patties among four plates and serve warm.

Homemade Fish Sticks (Air Fryer)

Prep time: 10 minutes | Cook time: 6 to 8 minutes | Makes 8 fish sticks

- 8 ounces (227 g) fish fillets (pollock or cod), cut into ½×3-inch strips
- Salt, to taste (optional)
- ½ cup plain bread crumbs
- Cooking spray

1. Preheat the air fryer to 390ºF (199ºC).
2. Season the fish strips with salt to taste, if desired.
3. Place the bread crumbs on a plate. Roll the fish strips in the bread crumbs to coat. Spritz the fish strips with cooking spray.
4. Arrange the fish strips in the air fryer basket in a single layer and air fry for 6 to 8 minutes or until golden brown.
5. Cool for 5 minutes before serving.

Parmesan-Crusted Hake with Garlic Sauce (Air Fryer)

Prep time: 5 minutes | Cook time: 10 minutes | Serves 3

Fish:
- 6 tablespoons mayonnaise
- 1 tablespoon fresh lime juice
- 1 teaspoon Dijon mustard
- 1 cup grated Parmesan cheese
- Salt, to taste
- ¼ teaspoon ground black pepper, or more to taste
- 3 hake fillets, patted dry
- Nonstick cooking spray

Garlic Sauce:
- ¼ cup plain Greek yogurt
- 2 tablespoons olive oil
- 2 cloves garlic, minced
- ½ teaspoon minced tarragon leaves

1. Preheat the air fryer to 395ºF (202ºC).
2. Mix the mayo, lime juice, and mustard in a shallow bowl and whisk to combine. In another shallow bowl, stir together the grated Parmesan cheese, salt, and pepper.
3. Dredge each fillet in the mayo mixture, then roll them in the cheese mixture until they are evenly coated on both sides.
4. Spray the air fryer basket with nonstick cooking spray. Arrange the fillets in the basket and air fry for 10 minutes, or until the fish flakes easily with a fork. Flip the fillets halfway through the cooking time.
5. Meanwhile, in a small bowl, whisk all the ingredients for the sauce until well incorporated.
6. Serve the fish warm alongside the sauce.

Paprika Shrimp (Air Fryer)

Prep time: 5 minutes | Cook time: 10 minutes | Serves 4

* 1 pound (454 g) tiger shrimp
* 2 tablespoons olive oil
* ½ tablespoon old bay seasoning
* ¼ tablespoon smoked paprika
* ¼ teaspoon cayenne pepper
* A pinch of sea salt

1. Preheat the air fryer to 380ºF (193ºC).
2. Toss all the ingredients in a large bowl until the shrimp are evenly coated.
3. Arrange the shrimp in the air fryer basket and air fry for 10 minutes, shaking the basket halfway through, or until the shrimp are pink and cooked through.
4. Serve hot.

Garlicky Cod Fillets (Air Fryer)

Prep time: 10 minutes | Cook time: 10 to 12 minutes | Serves 4

* 1 teaspoon olive oil
* 4 cod fillets
* ¼ teaspoon fine sea salt
* ¼ teaspoon ground black pepper, or more to taste
* 1 teaspoon cayenne pepper
* ½ cup fresh Italian parsley,
* coarsely chopped
* ½ cup nondairy milk
* 1 Italian pepper, chopped
* 4 garlic cloves, minced
* 1 teaspoon dried basil
* ½ teaspoon dried oregano

1. Lightly coat the sides and bottom of a baking dish with the olive oil. Set aside.
2. In a large bowl, sprinkle the fillets with salt, black pepper, and cayenne pepper.
3. In a food processor, pulse the remaining ingredients until smoothly puréed.
4. Add the purée to the bowl of fillets and toss to coat, then transfer to the prepared baking dish.
5. Preheat the air fryer to 380ºF (193ºC).
6. Put the baking dish in the air fryer basket and bake for 10 to 12 minutes, or until the fish flakes when pressed lightly with a fork.
7. Remove from the basket and serve warm.

Easy Scallops (Air Fryer)

Prep time: 5 minutes | Cook time: 4 minutes | Serves 2

* 12 medium sea scallops, rinsed and patted dry
* 1 teaspoon fine sea salt
* ¾ teaspoon ground black pepper,

* plus more for garnish
* Fresh thyme leaves, for garnish (optional)
* Avocado oil spray

1. Preheat the air fryer to 390ºF (199ºC). Coat the air fryer basket with avocado oil spray.
2. Place the scallops in a medium bowl and spritz with avocado oil spray. Sprinkle the salt and pepper to season.
3. Transfer the seasoned scallops to the air fryer basket, spacing them apart. You may need to work in batches to avoid overcrowding.
4. Air fry for 4 minutes, flipping the scallops halfway through, or until the scallops are firm and reach an internal temperature of just 145ºF (63ºC) on a meat thermometer.
5. Remove from the basket and repeat with the remaining scallops.
6. Sprinkle the pepper and thyme leaves on top for garnish, if desired. Serve immediately.

Parmesan Fish Fillets (Air Fryer)

Prep time: 8 minutes | Cook time: 17 minutes | Serves 4

* ⅓ cup grated Parmesan cheese
* ½ teaspoon fennel seed
* ½ teaspoon tarragon
* ⅓ teaspoon mixed peppercorns
* 2 eggs, beaten

* 4 (4-ounce / 113-g) fish fillets, halved
* 2 tablespoons dry white wine
* 1 teaspoon seasoned salt

1. Preheat the air fryer to 345ºF (174ºC).
2. Place the grated Parmesan cheese, fennel seed, tarragon, and mixed peppercorns in a food processor and pulse for about 20 seconds until well combined. Transfer the cheese mixture to a shallow dish.
3. Place the beaten eggs in another shallow dish.
4. Drizzle the dry white wine over the top of fish fillets. Dredge each fillet in the beaten eggs on both sides, shaking off any excess, then roll them in the cheese mixture until fully coated. Season with the salt.
5. Arrange the fillets in the air fryer basket and air fry for about 17 minutes, or until the fish is cooked through and no longer translucent. Flip the fillets once halfway through the cooking time.
6. Cool for 5 minutes before serving.

Cajun and Lemon Pepper Cod (Air Fryer)

Prep time: 5 minutes | Cook time: 12 minutes | Makes 2 cod fillets

❀ 1 tablespoon Cajun seasoning
❀ 1 teaspoon salt
❀ ½ teaspoon lemon pepper
❀ ½ teaspoon freshly ground black pepper
❀ 2 (8-ounce / 227-g) cod fillets, cut

to fit into the air fryer basket
❀ Cooking spray
❀ 2 tablespoons unsalted butter, melted
❀ 1 lemon, cut into 4 wedges

1. Preheat the air fryer to 360ºF (182ºC). Spritz the air fryer basket with cooking spray.
2. Thoroughly combine the Cajun seasoning, salt, lemon pepper, and black pepper in a small bowl. Rub this mixture all over the cod fillets until completely coated.
3. Put the fillets in the air fryer basket and brush the melted butter over both sides of each fillet.
4. Bake in the preheated air fryer for 12 minutes, flipping the fillets halfway through, or until the fish flakes easily with a fork.
5. Remove the fillets from the basket and serve with fresh lemon wedges.

Golden Beer-Battered Cod (Air Fryer)

Prep time: 5 minutes | Cook time: 15 minutes | Serves 4

❀ 2 eggs
❀ 1 cup malty beer
❀ 1 cup all-purpose flour
❀ ½ cup cornstarch

❀ 1 teaspoon garlic powder
❀ Salt and pepper, to taste
❀ 4 (4-ounce / 113-g) cod fillets
❀ Cooking spray

1. Preheat the air fryer to 400ºF (204ºC).
2. In a shallow bowl, beat together the eggs with the beer. In another shallow bowl, thoroughly combine the flour and cornstarch. Sprinkle with the garlic powder, salt, and pepper.
3. Dredge each cod fillet in the flour mixture, then in the egg mixture. Dip each piece of fish in the flour mixture a second time.
4. Spritz the air fryer basket with cooking spray. Arrange the cod fillets in the basket in a single layer.
5. Air fry in batches for 15 minutes until the cod reaches an internal temperature of 145ºF (63ºC) on a meat thermometer and the outside is crispy. Flip the fillets halfway through the cooking time.
6. Let the fish cool for 5 minutes and serve.

Chapter 8 Wraps and Sandwiches

Avocado and Tomato Egg Rolls (Air Fryer)

Prep time: 10 minutes | Cook time: 5 minutes | Serves 5

- 10 egg roll wrappers
- 3 avocados, peeled and pitted
- 1 tomato, diced
- Salt and ground black pepper, to taste
- Cooking spray

1. Preheat the air fryer to 350ºF (177ºC) and spritz with cooking spray.
2. Pu the tomato and avocados in a food processor. Sprinkle with salt and ground black pepper. Pulse to mix and coarsely mash until smooth.
3. Unfold the wrappers on a clean work surface, then divide the mixture in the center of each wrapper. Roll the wrapper up and press to seal.
4. Transfer the rolls in the preheated air fryer and spritz with cooking spray. Air fry for 5 minutes or until golden brown. Flip the rolls halfway through. Work in batches to avoid overcrowding.
5. Serve immediately.

Crispy Chicken Egg Rolls (Air Fryer)

Prep time: 10 minutes | Cook time: 23 to 24 minutes | Serves 4

- 1 pound (454 g) ground chicken
- 2 teaspoons olive oil
- 2 garlic cloves, minced
- 1 teaspoon grated fresh ginger
- 2 cups white cabbage, shredded
- 1 onion, chopped
- ¼ cup soy sauce
- 8 egg roll wrappers
- 1 egg, beaten
- Cooking spray

1. Preheat the air fryer to 370ºF (188ºC). Spritz the air fryer basket with cooking spray.
2. Heat olive oil in a saucepan over medium heat. Sauté the garlic and ginger in the olive oil for 1 minute, or until fragrant. Add the ground chicken to the saucepan. Sauté for 5 minutes, or until the chicken is cooked through. Add the cabbage, onion and soy sauce and sauté for 5 to 6 minutes, or until the vegetables become soft. Remove the saucepan from the heat.
3. Unfold the egg roll wrappers on a clean work surface. Divide the chicken mixture among the wrappers and brush the edges of the wrappers with the beaten egg. Tightly roll up the egg rolls, enclosing the filling.
4. Arrange the rolls in the prepared air fryer basket and air fry for 12 minutes, or until crispy and golden brown. Turn halfway through the cooking time to ensure even cooking.
5. Transfer to a platter and let cool for 5 minutes before serving.

Golden Cod Tacos with Salsa (Air Fryer)

Prep time: 5 minutes | Cook time: 15 minutes | Serves 4

- ❁ 2 eggs
- ❁ 1¼ cups Mexican beer
- ❁ 1½ cups coconut flour
- ❁ 1½ cups almond flour
- ❁ ½ tablespoon chili powder
- ❁ 1 tablespoon cumin
- ❁ Salt, to taste
- ❁ 1 pound (454 g) cod fillet, slice into large pieces
- ❁ 4 toasted corn tortillas
- ❁ 4 large lettuce leaves, chopped
- ❁ ¼ cup salsa
- ❁ Cooking spray

1. Preheat the air fryer to 375ºF (191ºC). Spritz the air fryer basket with cooking spray.
2. Break the eggs in a bowl, then pour in the beer. Whisk to combine well.
3. Combine the coconut flour, almond flour, chili powder, cumin, and salt in a separate bowl. Stir to mix well.
4. Dunk the cod pieces in the egg mixture, then shake the excess off and dredge into the flour mixture to coat well.
5. Arrange the cod in the preheated air fryer. Air fry for 15 minutes or until golden brown. Flip the cod halfway through the cooking time.
6. Unwrap the toasted tortillas on a large plate, then divide the cod and lettuce leaves on top. Baste with salsa and wrap to serve.

Eggplant Hoagies (Air Fryer)

Prep time: 15 minutes | Cook time: 12 minutes | Makes 3 hoagies

- ❁ 6 peeled eggplant slices (about ½ inch thick and 3 inches in diameter)
- ❁ ¼ cup jarred pizza sauce
- ❁ 6 tablespoons grated Parmesan
- cheese
- ❁ 3 Italian sub rolls, split open lengthwise, warmed
- ❁ Cooking spray

1. Preheat the air fryer to 350ºF (177ºC) and spritz with cooking spray.
2. Arrange the eggplant slices in the preheated air fryer and spritz with cooking spray.
3. Air fry for 10 minutes or until lightly wilted and tender. Flip the slices halfway through.
4. Divide and spread the pizza sauce and cheese on top of the eggplant slice and air fry over 375ºF (191ºC) for 2 more minutes or until the cheese melts.
5. Assemble each sub roll with two slices of eggplant and serve immediately.

Lamb and Feta Hamburgers (Air Fryer)

Prep time: 15 minutes | Cook time: 16 minutes | Makes 4 burgers

* 1½ pounds (680 g) ground lamb
* ¼ cup crumbled feta
* 1½ teaspoons tomato paste
* 1½ teaspoons minced garlic
* 1 teaspoon ground dried ginger
* 1 teaspoon ground coriander
* ¼ teaspoon salt
* ¼ teaspoon cayenne pepper
* 4 kaiser rolls or hamburger buns, split open lengthwise, warmed
* Cooking spray

1. Preheat the air fryer to 375ºF (191ºC) and spritz with cooking spray.
2. Combine all the ingredients, except for the buns, in a large bowl. Coarsely stir to mix well.
3. Shape the mixture into four balls, then pound the balls into four 5-inch diameter patties.
4. Arrange the patties in the preheated air fryer and spritz with cooking spray. Air fry for 16 minutes or until well browned. Flip the patties halfway through.
5. Assemble the buns with patties to make the burgers and serve immediately.

Crispy Tilapia Tacos (Air Fryer)

Prep time: 20 minutes | Cook time: 10 minutes | Serves 4

* 2 tablespoons milk
* $1/3$ cup mayonnaise
* ¼ teaspoon garlic powder
* 1 teaspoon chili powder
* 1½ cups panko bread crumbs
* ½ teaspoon salt
* 4 teaspoons canola oil
* 1 pound (454 g) skinless tilapia fillets, cut into 3-inch-long and 1-inch-wide strips
* 4 small flour tortillas
* Lemon wedges, for topping
* Cooking spray

1. Preheat the air fryer to 400ºF (204ºC). Spritz the air fryer basket with cooking spray.
2. Combine the milk, mayo, garlic powder, and chili powder in a bowl. Stir to mix well. Combine the panko with salt and canola oil in a separate bowl. Stir to mix well.
3. Dredge the tilapia strips in the milk mixture first, then dunk the strips in the panko mixture to coat well. Shake the excess off.
4. Arrange the tilapia strips in the preheated air fryer. Air fry for 5 minutes or until opaque on all sides and the panko is golden brown. Flip the strips halfway through. You may need to work in batches to avoid overcrowding.
5. Unfold the tortillas on a large plate, then divide the tilapia strips over the tortillas. Squeeze the lemon wedges on top before serving.

Cheesy Potato Taquitos (Air Fryer)

Prep time: 5 minutes | Cook time: 6 minutes | Makes 12 taquitos

* 2 cups mashed potatoes
* ½ cup shredded Mexican cheese
* 12 corn tortillas
* Cooking spray

1. Preheat the air fryer to 400ºF (204ºC). Line the baking pan with parchment paper.
2. In a bowl, combine the potatoes and cheese until well mixed. Microwave the tortillas on high heat for 30 seconds, or until softened. Add some water to another bowl and set alongside.
3. On a clean work surface, lay the tortillas. Scoop 3 tablespoons of the potato mixture in the center of each tortilla. Roll up tightly and secure with toothpicks if necessary.
4. Arrange the filled tortillas, seam side down, in the prepared baking pan. Spritz the tortillas with cooking spray. Air fry for 6 minutes, or until crispy and golden brown, flipping once halfway through the cooking time. You may need to work in batches to avoid overcrowding.
5. Serve hot.

Beef and Bell Pepper Fajitas (Air Fryer)

Prep time: 15 minutes | Cook time: 10 minutes | Serves 4

* 1 pound (454 g) beef sirloin steak, cut into strips
* 2 shallots, sliced
* 1 orange bell pepper, sliced
* 1 red bell pepper, sliced
* 2 garlic cloves, minced
* 2 tablespoons Cajun seasoning
* 1 tablespoon paprika
* Salt and ground black pepper, to taste
* 4 corn tortillas
* ½ cup shredded Cheddar cheese
* Cooking spray

1. Preheat the air fryer to 360ºF (182ºC) and spritz with cooking spray.
2. Combine all the ingredients, except for the tortillas and cheese, in a large bowl. Toss to coat well.
3. Pour the beef and vegetables in the preheated air fryer and spritz with cooking spray.
4. Air fry for 10 minutes or until the meat is browned and the vegetables are soft and lightly wilted. Shake the basket halfway through.
5. Unfold the tortillas on a clean work surface and spread the cooked beef and vegetables on top. Scatter with cheese and fold to serve.

Mexican Flavor Chicken Burgers (Air Fryer)

Prep time: 15 minutes | Cook time: 20 minutes | Serves 6 to 8

- 4 skinless and boneless chicken breasts
- 1 small head of cauliflower, sliced into florets
- 1 jalapeño pepper
- 3 tablespoons smoked paprika
- 1 tablespoon thyme
- 1 tablespoon oregano
- 1 tablespoon mustard powder
- 1 teaspoon cayenne pepper
- 1 egg
- Salt and ground black pepper, to taste
- 2 tomatoes, sliced
- 2 lettuce leaves, chopped
- 6 to 8 brioche buns, sliced lengthwise
- ¾ cup taco sauce
- Cooking spray

1. Preheat the air fryer to 350ºF (177ºC) and spritz with cooking spray.
2. In a blender, add the cauliflower florets, jalapeño pepper, paprika, thyme, oregano, mustard powder and cayenne pepper and blend until the mixture has a texture similar to bread crumbs.
3. Transfer ¾ of the cauliflower mixture to a medium bowl and set aside. Beat the egg in a different bowl and set aside.
4. Add the chicken breasts to the blender with remaining cauliflower mixture. Sprinkle with salt and pepper. Blend until finely chopped and well mixed.
5. Remove the mixture from the blender and form into 6 to 8 patties. One by one, dredge each patty in the reserved cauliflower mixture, then into the egg. Dip them in the cauliflower mixture again for additional coating.
6. Place the coated patties into the air fryer basket and spritz with cooking spray. Air fry for 20 minutes or until golden and crispy. Flip halfway through to ensure even cooking.
7. Transfer the patties to a clean work surface and assemble with the buns, tomato slices, chopped lettuce leaves and taco sauce to make burgers. Serve and enjoy.

Korean Flavor Beef and Onion Tacos (Air Fryer)

Prep time: 1 hour 15 minutes | Cook time: 12 minutes | Serves 6

- 2 tablespoons gochujang
- 1 tablespoon soy sauce
- 2 tablespoons sesame seeds
- 2 teaspoons minced fresh ginger
- 2 cloves garlic, minced
- 2 tablespoons toasted sesame oil
- 2 teaspoons sugar
- ½ teaspoon kosher salt
- 1½ pounds (680 g) thinly sliced beef chuck
- 1 medium red onion, sliced
- 6 corn tortillas, warmed
- ¼ cup chopped fresh cilantro
- ½ cup kimchi
- ½ cup chopped green onions

1. Combine the gochujang, soy sauce, sesame seeds, ginger, garlic, sesame oil, sugar, and salt in a large bowl. Stir to mix well.
2. Dunk the beef chunk in the large bowl. Press to submerge, then wrap the bowl in plastic and refrigerate to marinate for at least 1 hour.
3. Preheat the air fryer to 400ºF (204ºC).
4. Remove the beef chunk from the marinade and transfer to the preheated air fryer basket. Add the onion and air fry for 12 minutes or until well browned. Shake the basket halfway through.
5. Unfold the tortillas on a clean work surface, then divide the fried beef and onion on the tortillas. Spread the cilantro, kimchi, and green onions on top.
6. Serve immediately.

Chapter 9 Appetizers and Snacks

Honey Carrots with Raisins (Pressure Cook)

Prep time: 5 minutes | Cook time: 5 minutes | Serves 3

- 1 pound (454 g) carrots, peeled and cut into chunks
- 2 tablespoons golden raisins
- ½ cup water
- ½ tablespoon honey
- ⅔ teaspoon crushed red pepper flakes
- ½ tablespoon melted butter
- Salt, to taste

1. Add the carrots, raisins, and water to the Instant Pot
2. Secure the lid and select the Pressure Cook. Set the cooking time for 5 minutes.
3. When the timer beeps, do a quick release, then open the lid.
4. Strain the carrots and transfer them to a large bowl.
5. Put the remaining ingredients into the bowl and toss well.
6. Serve warm.

Lentil and Beef Slider Patties (Pressure Cook)

Prep time: 25 minutes | Cook time: 25 minutes | Makes 15 patties

- 1 cup dried yellow lentils
- 2 cups beef broth
- ½ pound (227 g) 80/20 ground beef
- ½ cup chopped old-fashioned oats
- 2 large eggs, beaten
- 2 teaspoons Sriracha sauce
- 2 tablespoons diced yellow onion
- ½ teaspoon salt

1. Add the lentils and broth to the Instant Pot. Lock the lid.
2. Press the Pressure Cook and set the cook time for 15 minutes at High Pressure. When the timer beeps, let pressure release naturally for 10 minutes, then release any remaining pressure. Unlock the lid.
3. Transfer the lentils to a medium bowl with a slotted spoon. Smash most of the lentils with the back of a spoon until chunky.
4. Add beef, oats, eggs, Sriracha, onion, and salt. Whisk to combine them well. Form the mixture into 15 patties.
5. Cook in a skillet on stovetop over medium-high heat in batches for 10 minutes. Flip the patties halfway through.
6. Transfer patties to serving dish and serve warm.

Herbed Button Mushrooms (Pressure Cook)

Prep time: 10 minutes | Cook time: 4 minutes | Serves 4

- 6 ounces (170 g) button mushrooms, rinsed and drained
- 1 clove garlic, minced
- ½ cup vegetable broth
- ½ teaspoon dried basil
- ½ teaspoon onion powder
- ½ teaspoon dried oregano
- ⅓ teaspoon dried rosemary
- ½ teaspoon smoked paprika
- Coarse sea salt and ground black pepper, to taste
- 1 tablespoon tomato paste
- 1 tablespoon butter

1. Put all the ingredients, except for the tomato paste and butter, in the Instant Pot. Stir to mix well.
2. Secure the lid. Choose the Pressure Cook and set the cooking time for 4 minutes at High pressure.
3. Once cooking is complete, perform a quick pressure release. Carefully open the lid.
4. Stir in the tomato paste and butter. Serve immediately.

Sweet and Salty Snack Mix (Air Fryer)

Prep time: 5 minutes | Cook time: 10 to 12 minutes | Makes about 10 cups

- 3 tablespoons butter, melted
- ½ cup honey
- 1 teaspoon salt
- 2 cups granola
- 2 cups sesame sticks
- 2 cups crispy corn puff cereal
- 2 cups mini pretzel crisps
- 1 cup cashews
- 1 cup pepitas
- 1 cup dried cherries

1. In a small mixing bowl, mix together the butter, honey, and salt until well incorporated.
2. In a large bowl, put the granola, sesame sticks, corn puff cereal and pretzel crisps, cashews, and pepitas. Drizzle with the butter mixture and toss until evenly coated.
3. Preheat the air fryer to 370ºF (188ºC).
4. Transfer the snack mix to the air fryer basket. You may need to cook in batches depending on the size of your air fryer basket.
5. Air fry for 10 to 12 minutes until lightly toasted, shaking the basket a few times during cooking for even cooking
6. Remove from the basket and allow to cool completely. Repeat with the remaining snack mix.
7. Scatter with the dried cherries and mix well. Serve immediately.

Jalapeño Peanuts (Pressure Cook)

Prep time: 3 hours 20 minutes | Cook time: 45 minutes | Serves 4

- 4 ounces (113 g) raw peanuts in the shell
- 1 jalapeño, sliced
- 1 tablespoon Creole seasoning
- ½ tablespoon cayenne pepper
- ½ tablespoon garlic powder
- 1 tablespoon salt

1. Add all ingredients to the Instant Pot. Pour in enough water to cover. Stir to mix well. Use a steamer to gently press down the peanuts.
2. Secure the lid. Choose the Pressure Cook and set the cooking time for 45 minutes at High pressure.
3. Once cooking is complete, perform a natural pressure release for 15 minutes, then release any remaining pressure. Carefully open the lid.
4. Transfer the peanut and the liquid in a bowl, then refrigerate for 3 hours before serving.

Sausage Balls with Cheese (Air Fryer)

Prep time: 10 minutes | Cook time: 10 to 11 minutes | Serves 8

- 12 ounces (340 g) mild ground sausage
- 1½ cups baking mix
- 1 cup shredded mild Cheddar
- cheese
- 3 ounces (85 g) cream cheese, at room temperature
- 1 to 2 tablespoons olive oil

1. Preheat the air fryer to 325ºF (163ºC). Line the air fryer basket with parchment paper.
2. Mix together the ground sausage, baking mix, Cheddar cheese, and cream cheese in a large bowl and stir to incorporate.
3. Divide the sausage mixture into 16 equal portions and roll them into 1-inch balls with your hands.
4. Arrange the sausage balls on the parchment, leaving space between each ball. You may need to work in batches to avoid overcrowding.
5. Brush the sausage balls with the olive oil. Bake for 10 to 11 minutes, shaking the basket halfway through, or until the balls are firm and lightly browned on both sides.
6. Remove from the basket to a plate and repeat with the remaining balls.
7. Serve warm.

Sweet Potato Fries with Mayonnaise (Air Fryer)

Prep time: 5 minutes | Cook time: 20 minutes | Serves 2 to 3

- 1 large sweet potato (about 1 pound / 454 g), scrubbed

Dipping Sauce:
- ¼ cup light mayonnaise
- ½ teaspoon sriracha sauce

- 1 teaspoon vegetable or canola oil
- Salt, to taste

- 1 tablespoon spicy brown mustard
- 1 tablespoon sweet Thai chili sauce

1. Preheat the air fryer to 200ºF (93ºC).
2. On a flat work surface, cut the sweet potato into fry-shaped strips about ¼ inch wide and ¼ inch thick. You can use a Food Slicer to slice the sweet potato quickly and uniformly.
3. In a medium bowl, drizzle the sweet potato strips with the oil and toss well.
4. Transfer to the air fryer basket and air fry for 10 minutes, shaking the basket twice during cooking.
5. Remove the air fryer basket and sprinkle with the salt and toss to coat.
6. Increase the air fryer temperature to 400ºF (204ºC) and air fry for an additional 10 minutes, or until the fries are crispy and tender. Shake the basket a few times during cooking.
7. Meanwhile, whisk together all the ingredients for the sauce in a small bowl.
8. Remove the sweet potato fries from the basket to a plate and serve warm alongside the dipping sauce.

Paprika Deviled Eggs (Air Fryer)

Prep time: 20 minutes | Cook time: 16 minutes | Serves 12

- 3 cups ice
- 12 large eggs
- ½ cup mayonnaise
- 10 hamburger dill pickle chips, diced
- ¼ cup diced onion

- 2 teaspoons salt
- 2 teaspoons yellow mustard
- 1 teaspoon freshly ground black pepper
- ½ teaspoon paprika

1. Preheat the air fryer to 250ºF (121ºC).
2. Put the ice in a large bowl.
3. Place the eggs in the air fryer basket and bake for 16 minutes.
4. Remove the eggs from the basket to the large bowl of ice to cool.
5. When cool enough to handle, peel the eggs. Slice them in half lengthwise and scoop out yolks into a small bowl. Stir in the mayonnaise, pickles, onion, salt, mustard, and pepper. Mash the mixture with a fork until well combined.
6. Fill each egg white half with 1 to 2 teaspoons of the egg yolk mixture.
7. Sprinkle the paprika on top and serve immediately.

Hush Puppies (Air Fryer)

Prep time: 45 minutes | Cook time: 10 minutes | Serves 12

- 1 cup self-rising yellow cornmeal
- ½ cup all-purpose flour
- 1 teaspoon sugar
- 1 teaspoon salt
- 1 teaspoon freshly ground black pepper
- 1 large egg
- $1/_3$ cup canned creamed corn
- 1 cup minced onion
- 2 teaspoons minced jalapeño pepper
- 2 tablespoons olive oil, divided

1. Thoroughly combine the cornmeal, flour, sugar, salt, and pepper in a large bowl.
2. Whisk together the egg and corn in a small bowl. Pour the egg mixture into the bowl of cornmeal mixture and stir to combine. Stir in the minced onion and jalapeño. Cover the bowl with plastic wrap and place in the refrigerator for 30 minutes.
3. Preheat the air fryer to 375ºF (191ºC). Line the air fryer basket with parchment paper and lightly brush it with 1 tablespoon of olive oil.
4. Scoop out the cornmeal mixture and form into 24 balls, about 1 inch.
5. Arrange the balls in the parchment paper-lined basket, leaving space between each ball.
6. Air fry in batches for 5 minutes. Shake the basket and brush the balls with the remaining 1 tablespoon of olive oil. Continue cooking for 5 minutes until golden brown.
7. Remove the balls (hush puppies) from the basket and serve on a plate.

Spiced Apple Chips (Air Fryer)

Prep time: 10 minutes | Cook time: 10 minutes | Serves 4

- 4 medium apples (any type will work), cored and thinly sliced
- ¼ teaspoon nutmeg
- ¼ teaspoon cinnamon
- Cooking spray

1. Preheat the air fryer to 360ºF (182ºC).
2. Place the apple slices in a large bowl and sprinkle the spices on top. Toss to coat.
3. Working in batches, place the apple slices in the air fryer basket in a single layer and spray them with cooking spray.
4. Air fry for 10 minutes, shaking the basket halfway through, or until the apple chips are crispy.
5. Transfer the apple chips to a paper towel-lined plate and rest for 5 minutes before serving.

Garlic Edamame (Air Fryer)

Prep time: 5 minutes | Cook time: 16 to 20 minutes | Serves 4

* 2 tablespoon olive oil, divided
* 1 (16-ounce / 454-g) bag frozen edamame in pods
* ½ teaspoon garlic salt
* ½ teaspoon salt
* ¼ teaspoon freshly ground black pepper
* ½ teaspoon red pepper flakes (optional)

1. Preheat the air fryer to 375ºF (191ºC). Grease the air fryer basket with 1 tablespoon of olive oil.
2. Place the edamame in a medium bowl and drizzle the remaining 1 tablespoon of olive oil over the top. Toss to coat well.
3. Stir together the garlic salt, salt, pepper, and red pepper flakes (if desired) in a small bowl. Pour the mixture into the bowl of edamame and toss until the edamame is fully coated.
4. Arrange the edamame in the greased basket. You may need to cook in batches to avoid overcrowding.
5. Air fry for 8 to 10 minutes, shaking the basket halfway through, or until the edamame is crisp.
6. Remove from the basket to a plate and repeat with the remaining edamame.
7. Serve warm.

Paprika Potato Chips (Air Fryer)

Prep time: 5 minutes | Cook time: 22 minutes | Serves 3

* 2 medium potatoes, preferably Yukon Gold, scrubbed
* Cooking spray
* 2 teaspoons olive oil
* ½ teaspoon garlic granules
* ¼ teaspoon paprika
* ¼ teaspoon plus ⅛ teaspoon sea salt
* ¼ teaspoon freshly ground black pepper
* Ketchup or hot sauce, for serving

1. Preheat the air fryer to 392ºF (200ºC). Spritz the air fryer basket with cooking spray.
2. On a flat work surface, cut the potatoes into ¼-inch-thick slices. Transfer the potato slices to a medium bowl, along with the olive oil, garlic granules, paprika, salt, and pepper and toss to coat well.
3. Put the potato slices in the air fryer basket and air fry for 22 minutes until tender and nicely browned. Shake the basket twice during the cooking process for even cooking.
4. Remove from the basket and serve alongside the ketchup for dipping.

Carrot Chips (Air Fryer)

Prep time: 15 minutes | Cook time: 8 to 10 minutes | Serves 4

❀ 1 tablespoon olive oil, plus more for greasing the basket
❀ 4 to 5 medium carrots, trimmed

and thinly sliced
❀ 1 teaspoon seasoned salt

1. Preheat the air fryer to 390°F (199°C). Grease the air fryer basket with the olive oil.
2. Toss the carrot slices with 1 tablespoon of olive oil and salt in a medium bowl until thoroughly coated.
3. Arrange the carrot slices in the greased basket. You may need to work in batches to avoid overcrowding.
4. Air fry for 8 to 10 minutes until the carrot slices are crisp-tender. Shake the basket once during cooking.
5. Transfer the carrot slices to a bowl and repeat with the remaining carrots.
6. Allow to cool for 5 minutes and serve.

Spicy Tortilla Chips (Air Fryer)

Prep time: 5 minutes | Cook time: 8 to 12 minutes | Serves 4

❀ ½ teaspoon ground cumin
❀ ½ teaspoon paprika
❀ ½ teaspoon chili powder
❀ ½ teaspoon salt

❀ Pinch cayenne pepper
❀ 8 (6-inch) corn tortillas, each cut into 6 wedges
❀ Cooking spray

1. Preheat the air fryer to 375°F (191°C). Lightly spritz the air fryer basket with cooking spray.
2. Stir together the cumin, paprika, chili powder, salt, and pepper in a small bowl.
3. Working in batches, arrange the tortilla wedges in the air fryer basket in a single layer. Lightly mist them with cooking spray. Sprinkle some seasoning mixture on top of the tortilla wedges.
4. Air fry for 4 to 6 minutes, shaking the basket halfway through, or until the chips are lightly browned and crunchy.
5. Repeat with the remaining tortilla wedges and seasoning mixture.
6. Let the tortilla chips cool for 5 minutes and serve.

Cheese and Ham Stuffed Baby Bella (Air Fryer)

Prep time: 15 minutes | Cook time: 12 minutes | Serves 8

* 4 ounces (113 g) Mozzarella cheese, cut into pieces
* ½ cup diced ham
* 2 green onions, chopped
* 2 tablespoons bread crumbs
* ½ teaspoon garlic powder
* ¼ teaspoon ground oregano
* ¼ teaspoon ground black pepper
* 1 to 2 teaspoons olive oil
* 16 fresh baby bella mushrooms, stemmed removed

1. Process the cheese, ham, green onions, bread crumbs, garlic powder, oregano, and pepper in a food processor until finely chopped.
2. With the food processor running, slowly drizzle in 1 to 2 teaspoons olive oil until a thick paste has formed. Transfer the mixture to a bowl.
3. Evenly divide the mixture into the mushroom caps and lightly press down the mixture.
4. Preheat the air fryer to 390ºF (199ºC).
5. Lay the mushrooms in the air fryer basket in a single layer. You'll need to work in batches to avoid overcrowding.
6. Roast for 12 minutes until the mushrooms are lightly browned and tender.
7. Remove from the basket to a plate and repeat with the remaining mushrooms.
8. Let the mushrooms cool for 5 minutes and serve warm.

Turkey Bacon-Wrapped Dates (Air Fryer)

Prep time: 10 minutes | Cook time: 5 to 7 minutes | Makes 16 appetizers

* 16 whole dates, pitted
* 16 whole almonds
* 6 to 8 strips turkey bacon, cut in half

Special Equipment:
* 16 toothpicks, soaked in water for at least 30 minutes

1. Preheat the air fryer to 390ºF (199ºC).
2. On a flat work surface, stuff each pitted date with a whole almond.
3. Wrap half slice of bacon around each date and secure it with a toothpick.
4. Place the bacon-wrapped dates in the air fryer basket and air fry for 5 to 7 minutes, or until the bacon is cooked to your desired crispiness.
5. Transfer the dates to a paper towel-lined plate to drain. Serve hot.

Easy Muffuletta Sliders with Olives (Air Fryer)

Prep time: 10 minutes | Cook time: 5 to 7 minutes | Makes 8 sliders

* ¼ pound (113 g) thinly sliced deli ham
* ¼ pound (113 g) thinly sliced pastrami
* 4 ounces (113 g) low-fat Mozzarella cheese, grated
* 8 slider buns, split in half
* Cooking spray
* 1 tablespoon sesame seeds

Olive Mix:

* ½ cup sliced green olives with pimentos
* ¼ cup sliced black olives
* ¼ cup chopped kalamata olives
* 1 teaspoon red wine vinegar
* ¼ teaspoon basil
* ⅛ teaspoon garlic powder

1. Preheat the air fryer to 360ºF (182ºC).
2. Combine all the ingredients for the olive mix in a small bowl and stir well.
3. Stir together the ham, pastrami, and cheese in a medium bowl and divide the mixture into 8 equal portions.
4. Assemble the sliders: Top each bottom bun with 1 portion of meat and cheese, 2 tablespoons of olive mix, finished by the remaining buns. Lightly spritz the tops with cooking spray. Scatter the sesame seeds on top.
5. Working in batches, arrange the sliders in the air fryer basket. Bake for 5 t0 7 minutes until the cheese melts.
6. Transfer to a large plate and repeat with the remaining sliders.
7. Serve immediately.

Chapter 10 Desserts

Cardamom Yogurt Pudding (Pressure Cook)

Prep time: 20 minutes | Cook time: 15 minutes | Serves 4

❀ 1½ cups Greek yogurt
❀ 1 teaspoon cocoa powder
❀ 2 cups sweetened condensed milk

❀ 1 teaspoon cardamom powder
❀ 1 cup water
❀ ¼ cup mixed nuts, chopped

1. Spritz 4 medium ramekins with cooking spray. Set aside.
2. In a bowl, combine the Greek yogurt, cocoa powder, condensed milk, and cardamom powder. Pour mixture into ramekins and cover with foil.
3. Pour the water into the Instant Pot, then fit in a trivet, and place ramekins on top.
4. Seal the lid, select the Pressure Cook and set the cooking time for 15 minutes at High Pressure.
5. When cooking is complete, perform a natural pressure release for 15 minutes, then release any remaining pressure. Unlock the lid.
6. Remove the ramekins from the pot, then take off the foil. Top with mixed nuts and serve immediately.

Classic Cheesecake (Pressure Cook)

Prep time: 3 hours 40 minutes | Cook time: 40 minutes | Serves 4

❀ 2 cups graham crackers, crushed
❀ 3 tablespoons brown sugar
❀ ¼ cup butter, melted
❀ 2 (8 ounce / 227-g) cream cheese, softened
❀ ½ cup granulated sugar

❀ 2 tablespoons all-purpose flour
❀ 1 teaspoon vanilla extract
❀ 3 eggs
❀ 1 cup water
❀ 1 cup caramel sauce

1. Make the crust: Mix the crushed crackers with brown sugar and butter. Spread the mixture at the bottom of a springform pan and use a spoon to press to fit. Freeze in refrigerator for 10 minutes.
2. In a bowl, whisk the cream cheese and sugar until smooth. Mix in the flour and vanilla. Whisk in the eggs. Remove the pan from refrigerator and pour mixture over crust. Cover the pan with foil.
3. Pour the water in Instant Pot, then fit in a trivet and place the pan on top.
4. Seal the lid, select the Pressure Cook and set the timer for 40 minutes at High Pressure.
5. When cooking is complete, allow a natural pressure release for 10 minutes, then release any remaining pressure. Open the lid.
6. Carefully remove the cake pan and take off the foil. Let cool for 10 minutes. Pour the caramel sauce over and refrigerate for 3 hours.
7. Remove the pan from the refrigerator and invert the cheesecake on a plate. Slice and serve.

Coconut-Potato Pudding (Pressure Cook)

Prep time: 5 minutes | Cook time: 10 minutes | Serves 4

- 1 cup water
- 1 large sweet potato (about 1 pound / 454 g), peeled and cut into 1-inch pieces
- ½ cup canned coconut milk
- 6 tablespoons pure maple syrup
- 1 teaspoon grated fresh ginger (about ½-inch knob)

1. Pour the water into the Instant Pot and fit in a steamer basket.
2. Place the sweet potato pieces in the steamer basket and secure the lid. Select the Pressure Cook and set the cooking time for 10 minutes at High Pressure.
3. When timer beeps, use a quick pressure release. Unlock the lid.
4. Transfer the cooked potatoes to a large bowl. Add the coconut milk, maple syrup, and ginger. Use an immersion blender to purée the potatoes into a smooth pudding.
5. Serve the pudding immediately or chill in the refrigerator for an hour before serving.

Creamy Banana Pudding (Pressure Cook)

Prep time: 5 minutes | Cook time: 5 minutes | Serves 4

- 1 cup whole milk
- 2 cups half-and-half
- ¾ cup plus 1 tablespoon granulated sugar, divided
- 4 egg yolks
- 3 tablespoon cornstarch
- 2 tablespoons cold butter, cut into 4 pieces
- 1 teaspoon vanilla extract
- 2 medium banana, peeled and sliced
- 1 cup heavy cream

1. Set the Instant Pot to Sauté mode. Mix the milk, half-and-half, and ½ cup of sugar in the pot.
2. Heat for 3 minutes or until sugar dissolves. Stir constantly.
3. Meanwhile, beat the egg yolks with ¼ cup of sugar in a medium bowl. Add cornstarch and mix well.
4. Scoop ½ cup of milk mixture into egg mixture and whisk until smooth. Pour mixture into Instant Pot.
5. Seal the lid, select the Pressure Cook and set the cooking time for 2 minutes at High Pressure.
6. When cooking is complete, do a quick pressure release and unlock the lid.
7. Stir in butter and vanilla. Lay banana pieces into 4 bowls and top with pudding.
8. In a bowl, whisk heavy cream with remaining sugar; spoon mixture on top of pudding. Refrigerate for 1 hour before serving.

Chocolate Oreo Cookie Cake (Pressure Cook)

Prep time: 8 hours 35 minutes | Cook time: 35 minutes | Serves 6

- ❀ 12 Oreo cookies, smoothly crushed
- ❀ 2 tablespoons salted butter, melted
- ❀ 16 ounces (454 g) cream cheese, softened
- ❀ ½ cup granulated sugar
- ❀ 2 large eggs
- ❀ 1 tablespoon all-purpose flour
- ❀ ¼ cup heavy cream
- ❀ 2 teaspoons vanilla extract
- ❀ 16 whole Oreo cookies, coarsely crushed
- ❀ 1½ cups water
- ❀ 1 cup whipped cream
- ❀ 2 tablespoons chocolate sauce, for topping

1. Line a springform pan with foil, then spritz with cooking spray.
2. Make the crust: In a bowl, combine smoothly crushed Oreo cookies with butter, then press into bottom of pan. Freeze for 15 minutes.
3. In another bowl, add cream cheese, and beat until smooth. Add sugar to whisk until satiny. Beat in the eggs one by one until mixed. Whisk in flour, heavy cream, and vanilla.
4. Fold in 8 coarsely crushed cookies and pour the mixture onto the crust in the springform pan. Cover pan tightly with foil.
5. Pour the water in the Instant Pot and fit in a trivet. Place the pan on trivet.
6. Seal the lid, set to the Pressure Cook and set the cooking time for 35 minutes at High Pressure.
7. When cooking is complete, allow a natural pressure release for 10 minutes, then release any remaining pressure. Carefully open the lid.
8. Remove the trivet with cake pan from the pot. Remove foil and transfer to a cooling rack to chill. Refrigerate for 8 hours. Top with whipped cream, remaining cookies, and chocolate sauce. Slice and serve.

Easy Orange Cake (Pressure Cook)

Prep time: 5 minutes | Cook time: 30 minutes | Serves 6

- ❀ 1½ cups orange soda
- ❀ 1 (15.25-ounce / 432-g) box orange cake mix
- ❀ 1 cup water
- ❀ 1 tablespoon caster sugar, for garnish

1. Spritz a bundt pan with cooking spray.
2. In a bowl, mix orange soda and orange cake mix until well combined. Pour into bundt pan, cover with a foil.
3. Pour the water in the Instant Pot, then fit in a trivet, and place the pan on top.
4. Seal the lid, select the Pressure Cook and set the cooking time for 30 minutes at High Pressure.
5. When cooking is complete, do a quick pressure release. Open the lid.
6. Remove the pan from the pot and allow cooling. Turn over onto a platter, sprinkle with caster sugar. Slice and serve.

Classic Pumpkin Pie (Pressure Cook)

Prep time: 4 hours 20 minutes | Cook time: 35 minutes | Serves 6

- ½ cup crushed graham crackers (about 7 graham crackers)
- 2 tablespoons unsalted butter, melted
- ½ cup brown sugar
- 1 large egg
- 1½ cups canned pumpkin purée
- 1½ teaspoons pumpkin pie spice
- ½ teaspoon sea salt
- ½ cup evaporated milk
- 1 cup water

1. Make the crust: In a small bowl, combine the graham cracker crumbs and butter and mix until well combined. Press the mixture into the bottom and 1 inch up the sides of a springform pan. Set aside.
2. In a large mixing bowl, whisk together the egg, pumpkin purée, pumpkin pie spice, sugar, salt, and milk. Pour the filling into the prepared crust. Cover the pan with aluminum foil.
3. Place a trivet in the Instant Pot and pour in the water. Lower the pan onto the trivet.
4. Lock the lid. Select the Pressure Cook. Set the time for 35 minutes at High Pressure.
5. When timer beeps, let the pressure release naturally for 10 minutes, then release the remaining pressure.
6. Unlock the lid. Remove the pan from the pot and then remove the foil. Allow the pie to cool. Cover with plastic wrap and refrigerate for at least 4 hours before serving.

Easy Bread Pudding (Pressure Cook)

Prep time: 15 minutes | Cook time: 25 minutes | Serves 8

- 2 cups milk
- 5 large eggs
- ⅓ cup granulated sugar
- 1 teaspoon vanilla extract
- 5 cups (about ½ loaf) bread, slice into 2-inch cubes
- 2 tablespoons unsalted butter, cut into small pieces

1. In a medium bowl, whisk together the eggs, milk, sugar, and vanilla. Add the bread cubes and stir to coat well. Refrigerate for 1 hour.
2. Spritz the Instant Pot with cooking spray. Pour in the bread mixture. Scatter with the butter pieces.
3. Lock the lid. Select the Pressure Cook. Set the timer for 25 minutes at High Pressure.
4. When timer beeps, let the pressure release naturally for 10 minutes, then release the remaining pressure. Unlock the lid.
5. Serve the pudding immediately or chill in the refrigerator for an hour before serving.

Oat and Raisin Cookie (Pressure Cook)

Prep time: 10 minutes | Cook time: 25 minutes | Serves 8

- ❀ ½ cup all-purpose flour
- ❀ ¼ teaspoon baking soda
- ❀ ½ cup sugar
- ❀ ¼ teaspoon fine sea salt
- ❀ 1 teaspoon ground cinnamon
- ❀ 1 egg

- ❀ ¼ cup melted butter
- ❀ ½ teaspoon pure vanilla extract
- ❀ ½ cup oats
- ❀ ½ cup raisins
- ❀ 1 cup water

1. Spritz a springform pan with cooking spray and line with parchment paper.
2. In a large bowl, stir together the flour, baking soda, sugar, salt, and cinnamon. Whisk in the egg, butter, and vanilla and stir until smooth.
3. Fold in the oats and raisins to make the batter thick and sticky. Transfer the batter to the prepared pan and use a spatula to smooth the top.
4. Pour the water into the Instant Pot and fit in a trivet on the bottom. Place the pan on top of the trivet and cover it with an upside-down plate.
5. Secure the lid. Select the Pressure Cook and set the cooking time for 25 minutes at High Pressure.
6. When timer beeps, let the pressure naturally release for 10 minutes, then release any remaining pressure. Unlock the lid.
7. Cut and serve.

Orange Toast (Pressure Cook)

Prep time: 10 minutes | Cook time: 15 minutes | Serves 4

- ❀ 2 large eggs
- ❀ 1 cup milk
- ❀ 2 teaspoons vanilla extract
- ❀ 1 teaspoon ground cinnamon

- ❀ Zest of 1 orange
- ❀ 6 bread slices, cubed
- ❀ 1 cup water
- ❀ Maple syrup, for topping

1. Beat the eggs with the milk, vanilla extract, cinnamon and orange zest in a mixing bowl.
2. Add the bread cubes and mix to coat. Pour the mixture into a greased baking pan and cover with aluminium foil.
3. Pour the water into the Instant Pot and fit in a trivet. Place the covered pan on top.
4. Seal the lid, select the Pressure Cook and set the cooking time for 15 minutes at High Pressure.
5. When cooking is complete, perform a quick pressure release. Unlock the lid, remove the pan, and take off the foil.
6. Let cool for 5 minutes. Drizzle with maple syrup to serve.

Chocolate Peppermint Cheesecake (Air Fryer)

Prep time: 5 minutes | Cook time: 18 minutes | Serves 6

Crust:
- ½ cup butter, melted
- ½ cup coconut flour
- 2 tablespoons stevia
- Cooking spray

Topping:
- 4 ounces (113 g) unsweetened baker's chocolate
- 1 cup mascarpone cheese, at room temperature
- 1 teaspoon vanilla extract
- 2 drops peppermint extract

1. Preheat the air fryer to 350ºF (177ºC). Lightly coat a baking pan with cooking spray.
2. In a mixing bowl, whisk together the butter, flour, and stevia until well combined. Transfer the mixture to the prepared baking pan.
3. Place the baking pan in the air fryer and bake for 18 minutes until a toothpick inserted in the center comes out clean.
4. Remove the crust from the air fryer to a wire rack to cool.
5. Once cooled completely, place it in the freezer for 20 minutes.
6. When ready, combine all the ingredients for the topping in a small bowl and stir to incorporate.
7. Spread this topping over the crust and let it sit for another 15 minutes in the freezer.
8. Serve chilled.

Simple Strawberry Pancake Bites (Pressure Cook)

Prep time: 15 minutes | Cook time: 10 minutes | Serves 4

- ½ cup fresh strawberries, chopped
- 2 large eggs
- 1 cup pancake mix
- 1¾ cup water, divided
- ¼ cup olive oil

1. In a medium bowl, combine strawberries, eggs, pancake mix, ¾ cup of water, and olive oil. Spoon the mixture into 4 muffin cups and cover with foil.
2. Pour 1 cup of water in Instant Pot, fit in a trivet, and place muffin cups on top.
3. Seal the lid, select the Pressure Cook and set the timer to 10 minutes at High Pressure.
4. When cooking is complete, allow a natural release for 10 minutes, then release any remaining pressure.
5. Unlock the lid, carefully remove cups, and take off the foil. Transfer the pancake bites onto plates and serve.

Pecan, Date, Sultana Stuffed Apples (Pressure Cook)

Prep time: 10 minutes | Cook time: 3 minutes | Serves 6

* ¼ cup toasted pecans, chopped
* ½ cup dates, chopped
* ¼ cup sultanas
* 1 tablespoon cinnamon powder
* 2 tablespoons brown sugar
* 4 tablespoons butter
* 6 red apples, whole and cored
* 4 tablespoons chocolate sauce, for topping

1. In a bowl, mix the pecans, dates, sultanas, cinnamon, brown sugar, and butter. Stuff apples with mixture.
2. Pour 1 cup of water in Instant Pot and place stuffed apples in water. Seal the lid, select the Pressure Cook and set the timer for 3 minutes at Low Pressure.
3. When cooking is complete, do a natural pressure release for 5 minutes, then release any remaining pressure. Open the lid.
4. Carefully remove apples onto plates and drizzle with chocolate sauce.

Chocolate and Rum Cupcakes (Air Fryer)

Prep time: 5 minutes | Cook time: 15 minutes | Serves 6

* ¾ cup granulated erythritol
* 1¼ cups almond flour
* 1 teaspoon unsweetened baking powder
* 3 teaspoons cocoa powder
* ½ teaspoon baking soda
* ½ teaspoon ground cinnamon
* ¼ teaspoon grated nutmeg
* ⅛ teaspoon salt
* ½ cup milk
* 1 stick butter, at room temperature
* 3 eggs, whisked
* 1 teaspoon pure rum extract
* ½ cup blueberries
* Cooking spray

1. Preheat the air fryer to 345ºF (174ºC). Spray a 6-cup muffin tin with cooking spray.
2. In a mixing bowl, combine the erythritol, almond flour, baking powder, cocoa powder, baking soda, cinnamon, nutmeg, and salt and stir until well blended.
3. In another mixing bowl, mix together the milk, butter, egg, and rum extract until thoroughly combined. Slowly and carefully pour this mixture into the bowl of dry mixture. Stir in the blueberries.
4. Spoon the batter into the greased muffin cups, filling each about three-quarters full.
5. Bake for 15 minutes, or until the center is springy and a toothpick inserted in the middle comes out clean.
6. Remove from the basket and place on a wire rack to cool. Serve immediately.

White Chocolate Cookies (Air Fryer)

Prep time: 5 minutes | Cook time: 11 minutes | Serves 10

- 8 ounces (227 g) unsweetened white chocolate
- 2 eggs, well beaten
- ¾ cup butter, at room temperature
- 1²/₃ cups almond flour
- ½ cup coconut flour
- ¾ cup granulated Swerve
- 2 tablespoons coconut oil
- ¹/₃ teaspoon grated nutmeg
- ¹/₃ teaspoon ground allspice
- ¹/₃ teaspoon ground anise star
- ¼ teaspoon fine sea salt

1. Preheat the air fryer to 350°F (177°C). Line the air fryer basket with parchment paper.
2. Combine all the ingredients in a mixing bowl and knead for about 3 to 4 minutes, or until a soft dough forms. Transfer to the refrigerator to chill for 20 minutes.
3. Make the cookies: Roll the dough into 1-inch balls and transfer to parchment-lined basket, spacing 2 inches apart. Flatten each with the back of a spoon.
4. Bake for about 11 minutes until the cookies are golden and firm to the touch.
5. Transfer to a wire rack and let the cookies cool completely. Serve immediately.

Yellow Pineapple Cake (Pressure Cook)

Prep time: 25 minutes | Cook time: 18 minutes | Serves 4

- 1 (18.5-ounce / 524-g) box yellow cake mix
- 2 tablespoons butter, melted
- ¼ cup brown sugar
- 1 cup pineapple slices
- 1 cup water

1. In a medium bowl, prepare the cake mix according to the instructions on box. Set aside.
2. Grease a springform pan with butter, sprinkle the brown sugar at the bottom of the pan and place the pineapple slices on top.
3. Pour the cake batter all over and cover the pan with foil. Pour the water in the Instant Pot, then fit in a trivet, and place the pan on top.
4. Seal the lid, select the Pressure Cook and set the timer for 18 minutes at High Pressure.
5. When cooking is complete, do a natural pressure release for 10 minutes, then release any remaining pressure.
6. Carefully remove cake pan, take off foil and let cool for 10 minutes. Turn cake over onto a plate. Slice and serve.

Chocolate and Coconut Cake (Air Fryer)

Prep time: 5 minutes | Cook time: 15 minutes | Serves 6

* ½ cup unsweetened chocolate, chopped
* ½ stick butter, at room temperature
* 1 tablespoon liquid stevia
* 1½ cups coconut flour

* 2 eggs, whisked
* ½ teaspoon vanilla extract
* A pinch of fine sea salt
* Cooking spray

1. Place the chocolate, butter, and stevia in a microwave-safe bowl. Microwave for about 30 seconds until melted.
2. Let the chocolate mixture cool for 5 to 10 minutes.
3. Add the remaining ingredients to the bowl of chocolate mixture and whisk to incorporate.
4. Preheat the air fryer to 330ºF (166ºC). Lightly spray a baking pan with cooking spray.
5. Scrape the chocolate mixture into the prepared baking pan.
6. Place the baking pan in the air fryer basket and bake for 15 minutes, or until the top springs back lightly when gently pressed with your fingers.
7. Let the cake cool for 5 minutes and serve.

Mixed Berries with Pecan Streusel Topping (Air Fryer)

Prep time: 5 minutes | Cook time: 17 minutes | Serves 3

* ½ cup mixed berries

Topping:
* 1 egg, beaten
* 3 tablespoons almonds, slivered
* 3 tablespoons chopped pecans
* 2 tablespoons chopped walnuts

* Cooking spray

* 3 tablespoons granulated Swerve
* 2 tablespoons cold salted butter, cut into pieces
* ½ teaspoon ground cinnamon

1. Preheat the air fryer to 340ºF (171ºC). Lightly spray a baking dish with cooking spray.
2. Make the topping: In a medium bowl, stir together the beaten egg, nuts, Swerve, butter, and cinnamon until well blended.
3. Put the mixed berries in the bottom of the baking dish and spread the topping over the top.
4. Bake in the preheated air fryer for 17 minutes, or until the fruit is bubbly and topping is golden brown.
5. Allow to cool for 5 to 10 minutes before serving.

Orange Coconut Cake (Air Fryer)

Prep time: 5 minutes | Cook time: 17 minutes | Serves 6

- 1 stick butter, melted
- ¾ cup granulated Swerve
- 2 eggs, beaten
- ¾ cup coconut flour
- ¼ teaspoon salt
- ⅓ teaspoon grated nutmeg
- ⅓ cup coconut milk
- 1¼ cups almond flour
- ½ teaspoon baking powder
- 2 tablespoons unsweetened orange jam
- Cooking spray

1. Preheat the air fryer to 355ºF (179ºC). Coat a baking pan with cooking spray. Set aside.
2. In a large mixing bowl, whisk together the melted butter and granulated Swerve until fluffy.
3. Mix in the beaten eggs and whisk again until smooth. Stir in the coconut flour, salt, and nutmeg and gradually pour in the coconut milk. Add the remaining ingredients and stir until well incorporated.
4. Scrape the batter into the baking pan.
5. Bake in the preheated air fryer for 17 minutes until the top of the cake springs back when gently pressed with your fingers.
6. Remove from the air fryer to a wire rack to cool. Serve chilled.

Classic Pound Cake (Air Fryer)

Prep time: 5 minutes | Cook time: 30 minutes | Serves 8

- 1 stick butter, at room temperature
- 1 cup Swerve
- 4 eggs
- 1½ cups coconut flour
- ½ cup buttermilk
- ½ teaspoon baking soda
- ½ teaspoon baking powder
- ¼ teaspoon salt
- 1 teaspoon vanilla essence
- A pinch of ground star anise
- A pinch of freshly grated nutmeg
- Cooking spray

1. Preheat the air fryer to 320ºF (160ºC). Spray a baking pan with cooking spray.
2. With an electric mixer or hand mixer, beat the butter and Swerve until creamy. One at a time, mix in the eggs and whisk until fluffy. Add the remaining ingredients and stir to combine.
3. Transfer the batter to the prepared baking pan. Bake in the preheated air fryer for 30 minutes until the center of the cake is springy. Rotate the pan halfway through the cooking time.
4. Allow the cake to cool in the pan for 10 minutes before removing and serving.

Lemon Ricotta Cake (Air Fryer)

Prep time: 5 minutes | Cook time: 25 minutes | Serves 6

* 17.5 ounces (496 g) ricotta cheese
* 5.4 ounces (153 g) sugar
* 3 eggs, beaten
* 3 tablespoons flour
* 1 lemon, juiced and zested
* 2 teaspoons vanilla extract

1. Preheat the air fryer to 320ºF (160ºC).
2. In a large mixing bowl, stir together all the ingredients until the mixture reaches a creamy consistency.
3. Pour the mixture into a baking pan and place in the air fryer.
4. Bake for 25 minutes until a toothpick inserted in the center comes out clean.
5. Allow to cool for 10 minutes on a wire rack before serving.

Air Fryer Apple Fritters

Prep time: 30 minutes | Cook time: 7 to 8 minutes | Serves 6

* 1 cup chopped, peeled Granny Smith apple
* ½ cup granulated sugar
* 1 teaspoon ground cinnamon
* 1 cup all-purpose flour
* 1 teaspoon baking powder
* 1 teaspoon salt
* 2 tablespoons milk
* 2 tablespoons butter, melted
* 1 large egg, beaten
* Cooking spray
* ¼ cup confectioners' sugar (optional)

1. Mix together the apple, granulated sugar, and cinnamon in a small bowl. Allow to sit for 30 minutes.
2. Combine the flour, baking powder, and salt in a medium bowl. Add the milk, butter, and egg and stir to incorporate.
3. Pour the apple mixture into the bowl of flour mixture and stir with a spatula until a dough forms.
4. Make the fritters: On a clean work surface, divide the dough into 12 equal portions and shape into 1-inch balls. Flatten them into patties with your hands.
5. Preheat the air fryer to 350ºF (177ºC). Line the air fryer basket with parchment paper and spray it with cooking spray.
6. Transfer the apple fritters onto the parchment paper, evenly spaced but not too close together. Spray the fritters with cooking spray.
7. Bake for 7 to 8 minutes until lightly browned. Flip the fritters halfway through the cooking time.
8. Remove from the basket to a plate and serve with the confectioners' sugar sprinkled on top, if desired.
9.

Blackberry Chocolate Cake (Air Fryer)

Prep time: 10 minutes | Cook time: 22 minutes | Serves 8

- ½ cup butter, at room temperature
- 2 ounces (57 g) Swerve
- 4 eggs
- 1 cup almond flour
- 1 teaspoon baking soda
- $1/_3$ teaspoon baking powder
- ½ cup cocoa powder
- 1 teaspoon orange zest
- $1/_3$ cup fresh blackberries

1. Preheat the air fryer to 335ºF (168ºC).
2. With an electric mixer or hand mixer, beat the butter and Swerve until creamy.
3. One at a time, mix in the eggs and beat again until fluffy.
4. Add the almond flour, baking soda, baking powder, cocoa powder, orange zest and mix well. Add the butter mixture to the almond flour mixture and stir until well blended. Fold in the blackberries.
5. Scrape the batter to a baking pan and bake in the preheated air fryer for 22 minutes. Check the cake for doneness: If a toothpick inserted into the center of the cake comes out clean, it's done.
6. Allow the cake cool on a wire rack to room temperature. Serve immediately.

Fudgy Cocoa Brownies (Air Fryer)

Prep time: 5 minutes | Cook time: 20 to 22 minutes | Serves 8

- 1 stick butter, melted
- 1 cup Swerve
- 2 eggs
- 1 cup coconut flour
- ½ cup unsweetened cocoa powder
- 2 tablespoons flaxseed meal
- 1 teaspoon baking powder
- 1 teaspoon vanilla essence
- A pinch of salt
- A pinch of ground cardamom
- Cooking spray

1. Preheat the air fryer to 350ºF (177ºC). Spray a baking pan with cooking spray.
2. Beat together the melted butter and Swerve in a large mixing dish until fluffy. Whisk in the eggs.
3. Add the coconut flour, cocoa powder, flaxseed meal, baking powder, vanilla essence, salt, and cardamom and stir with a spatula until well incorporated. Spread the mixture evenly into the prepared baking pan.
4. Place the baking pan in the air fryer basket and bake for 20 to 22 minutes, or until a toothpick inserted in the center comes out clean.
5. Remove from the basket and place on a wire rack to cool completely. Cut into squares and serve immediately.

Peanut Butter and Chocolate Tart (Pressure Cook)

Prep time: 20 minutes | Cook time: 25 minutes | Serves 4 to 6

- 5 tablespoons unsalted butter
- 1 cup granulated sugar
- 2 tablespoons peanut butter
- 1 tablespoon vegetable oil
- ¼ cup chocolate chips
- ½ cup peanut butter chips
- 1/3 cup cocoa powder
- 2 large eggs
- 1 cup all-purpose flour
- 1 teaspoon baking powder
- 2 teaspoons vanilla extract
- ½ teaspoon salt
- 2 tablespoons water
- 5 ounces (142 g) chocolate chip cookie dough, rolled into teaspoon-size balls

1. Combine the butter, sugar, and peanut butter in a microwave-safe bowl and microwave for a minute to melt and mix well.
2. Add the vegetable oil to the bowl of butter mixture and whisk to combine.
3. Whisk in the remaining ingredients, except for the cookie dough balls.
4. Spritz a springform pan with cooking spray. Line the with parchment paper, then spritz with another layer of cooking spray.
5. Pour the mixture into the pan and use a spatula to level the top. Arrange the cookie-dough balls and slightly push them into the mixture and they're still visible on the surface.
6. Pour 2 cups of water in the Instant Pot, then fit in a trivet. Place the pan on the trivet.
7. Secure the lid, and select the Pressure Cook and set the cooking time for 25 minutes.
8. When cooking is complete, do a natural pressure release for 10 minutes, then release any remaining pressure. Open the lid.
9. Carefully remove the pan and trivet from the Instant Pot and let cool for 30 minutes before slicing and serving.

Appendix 1: Measurement Conversion Chart

US STANDARD	METRIC (APPROXIMATE)
1/8 teaspoon	0.5 mL
1/4 teaspoon	1 mL
1/2 teaspoon	2 mL
3/4 teaspoon	4 mL
1 teaspoon	5 mL
1 tablespoon	15 mL
1/4 cup	59 mL
1/2 cup	118 mL
3/4 cup	177 mL
1 cup	235 mL
2 cups	475 mL
3 cups	700 mL
4 cups	1 L

US STANDARD	US STANDARD (OUNCES)	METRIC (APPROXIMATE)
2 tablespoons	1 fl.oz.	30 mL
1/4 cup	2 fl.oz.	60 mL
1/2 cup	4 fl.oz.	120 mL
1 cup	8 fl.oz.	240 mL
1 1/2 cup	12 fl.oz.	355 mL
2 cups or 1 pint	16 fl.oz.	475 mL
4 cups or 1 quart	32 fl.oz.	1 L
1 gallon	128 fl.oz.	4 L

TEMPERATURES EQUIVALENTS

FAHRENHEIT(F)	CELSIUS(C) (APPROXIMATE)
225 °F	107 °C
250 °F	120 °C
275 °F	135 °C
300 °F	150 °C
325 °F	160 °C
350 °F	180 °C
375 °F	190 °C
400 °F	205 °C
425 °F	220 °C
450 °F	235 °C
475 °F	245 °C
500 °F	260 °C

WEIGHT EQUIVALENTS

US STANDARD	METRIC (APPROXIMATE)
1 ounce	28 g
2 ounces	57 g
5 ounces	142 g
10 ounces	284 g
15 ounces	425 g
16 ounces (1 pound)	455 g
1.5 pounds	680 g
2 pounds	907 g

Appendix 2: Instant Pot Cooking Timetable

Dried Beans, Legumes and Lentils

Dried Beans and Legume	Dry (Minutes)	Soaked (Minutes)
Soy beans	25 – 30	20 – 25
Scarlet runner	20 – 25	10 – 15
Pinto beans	25 – 30	20 – 25
Peas	15 – 20	10 – 15
Navy beans	25 – 30	20 – 25
Lima beans	20 – 25	10 – 15
Lentils, split, yellow (moong dal)	15 – 18	N/A
Lentils, split, red	15 – 18	N/A
Lentils, mini, green (brown)	15 – 20	N/A
Lentils, French green	15 – 20	N/A
Kidney white beans	35 – 40	20 – 25
Kidney red beans	25 – 30	20 – 25
Great Northern beans	25 – 30	20 – 25
Pigeon peas	20 – 25	15 – 20
Chickpeas (garbanzo bean chickpeas)	35 – 40	20 – 25
Cannellini beans	35 – 40	20 – 25
Black-eyed peas	20 – 25	10 – 15
Black beans	20 – 25	10 – 15

Fish and Seafood

Fish and Seafood	Fresh (minutes)	Frozen (minutes)
Shrimp or Prawn	1 to 2	2 to 3
Seafood soup or stock	6 to 7	7 to 9
Mussels	2 to 3	4 to 6
Lobster	3 to 4	4 to 6
Fish, whole (snapper, trout, etc.)	5 to 6	7 to 10
Fish steak	3 to 4	4 to 6
Fish fillet,	2 to 3	3 to 4
Crab	3 to 4	5 to 6

Fruits

Fruits	Fresh (in Minutes)	Dried (in Minutes)
Raisins	N/A	4 to 5
Prunes	2 to 3	4 to 5
Pears, whole	3 to 4	4 to 6
Pears, slices or halves	2 to 3	4 to 5
Peaches	2 to 3	4 to 5
Apricots, whole or halves	2 to 3	3 to 4
Apples, whole	3 to 4	4 to 6
Apples, in slices or pieces	2 to 3	3 to 4

Meat

Meat and Cuts	Cooking Time (minutes)	Meat and Cuts	Cooking Time (minutes)
Veal, roast	35 to 45	Duck, with bones, cut up	10 to 12
Veal, chops	5 to 8	Cornish Hen, whole	10 to 15
Turkey, drumsticks (leg)	15 to 20	Chicken, whole	20 to 25
Turkey, breast, whole, with bones	25 to 30	Chicken, legs, drumsticks, or thighs	10 to 15
Turkey, breast, boneless	15 to 20	Chicken, with bones, cut up	10 to 15
Quail, whole	8 to 10	Chicken, breasts	8 to 10
Pork, ribs	20 to 25	Beef, stew	15 to 20
Pork, loin roast	55 to 60	Beef, shanks	25 to 30
Pork, butt roast	45 to 50	Beef, ribs	25 to 30
Pheasant	20 to 25	Beef, steak, pot roast, round, rump, brisket or blade, small chunks, chuck,	25 to 30
Lamb, stew meat	10 to 15		
Lamb, leg	35 to 45	Beef, pot roast, steak, rump, round, chuck, blade or brisket, large	35 to 40
Lamb, cubes,	10 t0 15		
Ham slice	9 to 12	Beef, ox-tail	40 to 50
Ham picnic shoulder	25 to 30	Beef, meatball	10 to 15
Duck, whole	25 to 30	Beef, dressed	20 to 25

Vegetables (fresh/frozen)

Vegetable	Fresh (minutes)	Frozen (minutes)	Vegetable	Fresh (minutes)	Frozen (minutes)
Zucchini, slices or chunks	2 to 3	3 to 4	Mixed vegetables	2 to 3	3 to 4
Yam, whole, small	10 to 12	12 to 14	Leeks	2 to 4	3 to 5
Yam, whole, large	12 to 15	15 to 19	Greens (collards, beet greens, spinach, kale, turnip greens, swiss chard) chopped	3 to 6	4 to 7
Yam, in cubes	7 to 9	9 to 11			
Turnip, chunks	2 to 4	4 to 6	Green beans, whole	2 to 3	3 to 4
Tomatoes, whole	3 to 5	5 to 7	Escarole, chopped	1 to 2	2 to 3
Tomatoes, in quarters	2 to 3	4 to 5	Endive	1 to 2	2 to 3
Sweet potato, whole, small	10 to 12	12 to 14	Eggplant, chunks or slices	2 to 3	3 to 4
Sweet potato, whole, large	12 to 15	15 to 19	Corn, on the cob	3 to 4	4 to 5
Sweet potato, in cubes	7 to 9	9 to 11	Corn, kernels	1 to 2	2 to 3
Sweet pepper, slices or chunks	1 to 3	2 to 4	Collard	4 to 5	5 to 6
Squash, butternut, slices or chunks	8 to 10	10 to 12	Celery, chunks	2 to 3	3 to 4
Squash, acorn, slices or chunks	6 to 7	8 to 9	Cauliflower flowerets	2 to 3	3 to 4
Spinach	1 to 2	3 to 4	Carrots, whole or chunked	2 to 3	3 to 4
Rutabaga, slices	3 to 5	4 to 6	Carrots, sliced or shredded	1 to 2	2 to 3
Rutabaga, chunks	4 to 6	6 to 8	Cabbage, red, purple or green, wedges	3 to 4	4 to 5
Pumpkin, small slices or chunks	4 to 5	6 to 7	Cabbage, red, purple or green, shredded	2 to 3	3 to 4
Pumpkin, large slices or chunks	8 to 10	10 to 14	Brussel sprouts, whole	3 to 4	4 to 5
Potatoes, whole, large	12 to 15	15 to 19	Broccoli, stalks	3 to 4	4 to 5
Potatoes, whole, baby	10 to 12	12 to 14	Broccoli, flowerets	2 to 3	3 to 4
Potatoes, in cubes	7 to 9	9 to 11	Beets, small roots, whole	11 to 13	13 to 15
Peas, in the pod	1 to 2	2 to 3	Beets, large roots, whole	20 to 25	25 to 30
Peas, green	1 to 2	2 to 3	Beans, green/yellow or wax, whole, trim ends and strings	1 to 2	2 to 3
Parsnips, sliced	1 to 2	2 to 3			
Parsnips, chunks	2 to 4	4 to 6	Asparagus, whole or cut	1 to 2	2 to 3
Onions, sliced	2 to 3	3 to 4	Artichoke, whole, trimmed without leaves	9 to 11	11 to 13
Okra	2 to 3	3 to 4	Artichoke, hearts	4 to 5	5 to 6

Rice and Grains

Rice & Grain	Water Quantity (Grain: Water ratios)	Cooking Time (in Minutes)	Rice & Grain	Water Quantity (Grain: Water ratios)	Cooking Time (in Minutes)
Wheat berries	1:3	25 to 30	Oats, steel-cut	1:1	10
Spelt berries	1:3	15 to 20	Oats, quick cooking	1:1	6
Sorghum	1:3	20 to 25	Millet	1:1	10 to 12
Rice, wild	1:3	25 to 30	Kamut, whole	1:3	10 to 12
Rice, white	1:1.5	8	Couscous	1:2	5 to 8
Rice, Jasmine	1:1	4 to 10	Corn, dried, half	1:3	25 to 30
Rice, Brown	1:1.3	22 to 28	Congee, thin	1:6 ~ 1:7	15 to 20
Rice, Basmati	1:1.5	4 to 8	Congee, thick	1:4 ~ 1:5	15 to 20
Quinoa, quick cooking	1:2	8	Barley, pot	1:3 ~ 1:4	25 to 30
Porridge, thin	1:6 ~ 1:7	15 to 20	Barley, pearl	1:4	25 to 30

Appendix 3: Air Fryer Cooking Timetable

Beef

Item	Temp (°F)	Time (mins)	Item	Temp (°F)	Time (mins)
Beef Eye Round Roast (4 lbs.)	400 °F	45 to 55	Meatballs (1-inch)	370 °F	7
Burger Patty (4 oz.)	370 °F	16 to 20	Meatballs (3-inch)	380 °F	10
Filet Mignon (8 oz.)	400 °F	18	Ribeye, bone-in (1-inch, 8 oz)	400 °F	10 to 15
Flank Steak (1.5 lbs.)	400 °F	12	Sirloin steaks (1-inch, 12 oz)	400 °F	9 to 14
Flank Steak (2 lbs.)	400 °F	20 to 28			

Chicken

Item	Temp (°F)	Time (mins)	Item	Temp (°F)	Time (mins)
Breasts, bone in (1 ¼ lb.)	370 °F	25	Legs, bone-in (1 ¾ lb.)	380 °F	30
Breasts, boneless (4 oz)	380 °F	12	Thighs, boneless (1 ½ lb.)	380 °F	18 to 20
Drumsticks (2 ½ lb.)	370 °F	20	Wings (2 lb.)	400 °F	12
Game Hen (halved 2 lb.)	390 °F	20	Whole Chicken	360 °F	75
Thighs, bone-in (2 lb.)	380 °F	22	Tenders	360 °F	8 to 10

Pork & Lamb

Item	Temp (°F)	Time (mins)	Item	Temp (°F)	Time (mins)
Bacon (regular)	400 °F	5 to 7	Pork Tenderloin	370 °F	15
Bacon (thick cut)	400 °F	6 to 10	Sausages	380 °F	15
Pork Loin (2 lb.)	360 °F	55	Lamb Loin Chops (1-inch thick)	400 °F	8 to 12
Pork Chops, bone in (1-inch, 6.5 oz)	400 °F	12	Rack of Lamb (1.5 – 2 lb.)	380 °F	22

Fish & Seafood

Item	Temp (°F)	Time (mins)	Item	Temp (°F)	Time (mins)
Calamari (8 oz)	400 °F	4	Tuna Steak	400 °F	7 to 10
Fish Fillet (1-inch, 8 oz)	400 °F	10	Scallops	400 °F	5 to 7
Salmon, fillet (6 oz)	380 °F	12	Shrimp	400 °F	5
Swordfish steak	400 °F	10			

Vegetables					
INGREDIENT	AMOUNT	PREPARATION	OIL	TEMP	COOK TIME
Asparagus	2 bunches	Cut in half, trim stems	2 Tbsp	420°F	12-15 mins
Beets	1½ lbs	Peel, cut in ½-inch cubes	1Tbsp	390°F	28-30 mins
Bell peppers (for roasting)	4 peppers	Cut in quarters, remove seeds	1Tbsp	400°F	15-20 mins
Broccoli	1 large head	Cut in 1-2-inch florets	1Tbsp	400°F	15-20 mins
Brussels sprouts	1lb	Cut in half, remove stems	1Tbsp	425°F	15-20 mins
Carrots	1lb	Peel, cut in ¼-inch rounds	1 Tbsp	425°F	10-15 mins
Cauliflower	1 head	Cut in 1-2-inch florets	2 Tbsp	400°F	20-22 mins
Corn on the cob	7 ears	Whole ears, remove husks	1 Tbps	400°F	14-17 mins
Green beans	1 bag (12 oz)	Trim	1 Tbps	420°F	18-20 mins
Kale (for chips)	4 oz	Tear into pieces,remove stems	None	325°F	5-8 mins
Mushrooms	16 oz	Rinse, slice thinly	1 Tbps	390°F	25-30 mins
Potatoes, russet	1½ lbs	Cut in 1-inch wedges	1 Tbps	390°F	25-30 mins
Potatoes, russet	1lb	Hand-cut fries, soak 30 mins in cold water, then pat dry	½ -3 Tbps	400°F	25-28 mins
Potatoes, sweet	1lb	Hand-cut fries, soak 30 mins in cold water, then pat dry	1 Tbps	400°F	25-28 mins
Zucchini	1lb	Cut in eighths lengthwise, then cut in half	1 Tbps	400°F	15-20 mins

Appendix 4: Recipes Index

Made in the USA
Coppell, TX
16 January 2021